Davidson County Tennessee Deed Book H 1809–1821

Mary Sue Smith

HERITAGE BOOKS
2014

HERITAGE BOOKS

AN IMPRINT OF HERITAGE BOOKS, INC.

Books, CDs, and more—Worldwide

For our listing of thousands of titles see our website
at
www.HeritageBooks.com

Published 2014 by
HERITAGE BOOKS, INC.
Publishing Division
5810 Ruatan Street
Berwyn Heights, Md. 20740

Heritage Books by the author:

Davidson County, Tennessee Deed Book H: 1809–1821

Davidson County, Tennessee Deed Book T and W: 1829–1835

*Davidson County, Tennessee Deed Book Z:
Personal Property Deeds, September 5, 1835–January 2, 1838*

*Superior Court of Law and Equity
Mero District of Tennessee, 1803–1805, Middle Tennessee*

*Superior Court of Law and Equity
Mero District of Tennessee, 1806–1809, Middle Tennessee*

*Superior Court of Law and Equity
Mero District of Tennessee, 1810–1813, Middle Tennessee*

International Standard Book Numbers
Paperbound: 978-0-7884-1481-7
Clothbound: 978-0-7884-6032-6

Table of Contents

DEED BOOK 'H'
1809 - 1821

This Abstract of Deed Book 'H' is especially important in tracing African-American ancestry in early Middle Tennessee. It gives ownership of slaves and relationships in both white and black families. In many cases it is the only way to prove family relationships. An excellent example:

"Chloe and her increase, that were willed to my mother in law, Dorcas Becton by her father Sam'l Slade of North Carolina ...Chloe & increase are in the State of Georgia, being taken there by Samuel Slade Bector who is entitled to one seventh part of the whole increase.'

This found in Davidson County Tennessee records gives not only the members of the family in Davidson County Tennessee but where they emigrated from - where they went - and *most important* the maiden name of the mother of the Becton family!

I have left some of the original spelling and phrases to give a flavor of the period this book covers. This is usually found in the inventories of household goods. Many of the terms are unfamiliar & unused in our modern world -- *piggin - martingale, etc.,* but were of special importance in the household of the early 1800's.

Original page #'s are enclosed in [ ] at the end of each individual entry so the original entry may be located. Deed Book 'H' has been microfilmed and is included with the Davidson County Deed Books in major record repositories.

In the Index [*] denotes a free person of color and slaves are indexed under 'slave' and then alphabetically.

Mary Sue Smith
October 4, 1999

EWING, Alexander   Bill of Sale   Dec. 15, 1809
I, Joseph Dickson of Wilson County, have sold to Alexander Ewing of Davidson
County, TN four negro slaves; one woman named Nance, about twenty five years
old; one negro girl named Milly, about fifteen years old; one negro boy named
George, sixteen years old and one negro boy named Daniel, fifteen years old.
5 Sept 1809 Joseph Dickson Test: R. McGavock; J. L. Ewing
Oct Term 1809 Bill of Sale bet Joseph Dickson & Alex'dr Ewing was proved
in open court by the oaths of R. McGavock and John L. Ewing; ordered
registered this 15 Dec. 1809. Andrew Ewing, Clerk [p1]

WILCOX, Thomas   Bill of Sale   Dec. 16, 1809
I, Moses Brown on the 18th Feb. 1808, did sell to Thomas Wilcox a certain
negro boy named James, aged fifteen. Moses Brown
Test: Wm Bryant & Rich'd Fitzhugh
Oct. Term 1809 Bill of Sale bet Moses Brown & Thos Wilcox was proved by
oaths of Wm Bryant and Rick'd Fitzhugh; ordered registered this 16 Dec 1809
Andrew Ewing, Clerk [p1]

GOFF, Thomas   Bill of Sale   Dec. 16, 1809
I, Christopher Stump of Davidson County, have this day sold to Thomas Goff
of Smith County, TN a negro man slave named Isaac, about twenty two years
old. 23 Oct. 1809 C. Stump
Oct. Term 1809 Bill of Sale acknowledged by said Stump to be his act and
ordered registered this 28th day of Oct. 1809 Andrew Ewing, Clerk [p2]

PERRY, George   Bill of Sale   Dec. 16, 1809
We, Elizabeth Phillips & John S. Cox, adm. of Marvil Phillips, deceased of
Davidson County, have this day sold to George Perry a certain negro woman
named Phillis, aged fifteen years old this 19 day of Aug. 1809. Elizabeth
Phillips, Admrx Jno S. Cox, Admr Wit: R. Hyde, Richard Rapier
Oct. Term 1809 proven in open Court by the oaths of Richard Hyde & Richard
Rapier and ordered registered this 28th day of Oct. 1809. [p2]

STUMP, Christopher   Bill of Sale   Dec. 16, 1809
I, William Roberts of Davidson County have this day sold to Christopher Stump
of the same county a negro slave boy named Dave, about seventeen years old,
this 9th day of Nov. 1808 Wm Roberts Wit: Exum Johnston, Rich'd Rapier
Oct. Term 1809 Bill of Sale duly proven in open Court by the oaths of Exum
Johnston and Richard Rapier & ordered registered. Andrew Ewing, Clk [p3]

NICHOLS, John   Mortgage   Dec. 18, 1809
I, Washington Croft, have this day sold to John Nichols a negro man slave by
the name of Dick, aged about thirty years, on the following condition. Nichols
has bound himself as Security on a Bond for obtaining an Injunction in the Court
of Equity on a Judgment obtained by Benjamin Huneycutt agst said Washington
Croft. If said Washington shall pay and discharge the judgment and costs this
deed is of no effect. 15 March 1809 Washington Croft
Wt: B. Searcy, W. Carman
Oct. Sessions 1809 This Mortgage proven in open Court by the oath of Bennet
Searcy, one of the subscribing witnesses this 28th day of Oct. 1809 [p3]

BRADSHAW, William   Bill of Sale   Dec. 18, 1809
I, Thomas Hudson sell to William Bradshaw the following negroes: a negro man
named Davey about thirty four years old; a negro woman named Nancy, wife of
said Davey, about thirty years old; and said Nancy's three children, Jerry, Anny
and a sucking child, the name not known. 17 Oct. 1809 Thos Hudson
Oct. Term 1809 This Bill of Sale duly acknowledged in open Court by the said
Hudson to be his act and ordered registered. 28 Oct. 1809   [p4]

EWING, Alexander   Bill of Sale   Dec. 18, 1809
I, William Caldwell of Davidson County have sold to Alex'r Ewing a negro
woman slave named Lidia, about forty years old. 4 Aug 1809 Wm Caldwell
Wt: R. McGavock
Oct. Term 1809 This Bill of Sale acknowledged in open Court by the said
William Caldwell and ordered registered. Andrew Ewing, Clk   [p4]

RAGLAND, Henry   Bill of Sale   Dec. 18, 1809
I hereby sell to Henry Ragland, of the County of Montgomery, a negro man
named David, about twenty one years old. 13 Sept. 1809
Wm Hill   Test: John M. Goodloe
Oct. Term 1809 The Bill of sale William Hill to Henry Ragland proven in Open
Court by the oath of John M. Goodloe & ordered registered.   [p5]

WADE, Dabney   Bill of Sale   Dec. 18, 1809
I, Thomas Porter, of the County of Davidson, have sold unto Dabney Wade a
certain Stud Horse, known by the name of the Young McKinney Roan, which
was formerly the property of William Roberts.
17 Oct. 1809 Thos. Porter   Test: Geo. Patton
Oct. Term 1809 This Bill of Sale, Thomas Porter to Dabney Wade was
acknowledged in Open Court & ordered registered. 28 Oct. 1809   [p5]

2

NICHOLS, John   Bill of Sale   Dec. 18, 1809
I, Washington Croft, sell to John Nichols a certain negro man by the name of
Moses, about twenty eight years old. Whereas the said John Nichols on the 15th
March last Bound himself as Security in a Bond for obtaining an Injunction in
the Court of Equity on a judgment obtained by Benjamin Honeycutt against the
said Washington Croft. If Croft shall pay and discharge the Judgment and costs
this bill to be null & void. 5 Apr 1809 Wit: Hez'h Harris, Henry Ingram
Oct Term 1809 This Bill of Sale or Mortgage was duly proven in open Court
by the Oath of Hezekiah Morris, one of the subscribing witnesses. 28 Oct. 1809
Andrew Ewing, Clk   [p6]

ROAD, John   Bill of Sale   Dec. 18, 1809
I hereby sell to John Road a certain Negro girl now in the possession of William
Cox, by the name of Ginney. 7 Oct. 1808   Andrew Hamilton
Test: Michael Molton
Oct. Term 1809 This Bill of Sale proven in open Court by the oath of Michael
Molton & ordered registered. 28 Oct. 1809 Andrew Ewing, Clk   [p6]

WEAKLEY, Robert   Bill of Sale   Jan. 30, 1809
I, Benjamin Drake, sell a certain negro man slave by the name of Tom, about
thirty three years old, to Robert Weakley. Jan. 30, 1809   Benjamin Drake
Test: Thomas Miles, John James
October Term 1809   Bill of Sale, Benjamin Drake to Robert Weakley
acknowledged in Open Court by the said Drake. 28 Oct. 1809   [p7]

DEMUMBRAUN, Timothy   Bill of Sale   Dec. 18, 1809
I have sold to Timothy Demumbraun a negro woman named Janey and her child,
Hartwell. 21 March 1808 Rich'd B. Owen Wit: John Gordon
October Term 1809   This Bill of Sale, Richard B. Owen to Timothy
Demumbraun, was duly acknowledged in Open Court by Owen & ordered
registered. 28 Oct 1809 Andrew Ewing   [p7]

McCORMACK, John   Bill of Sale   8 Nov. 1808
I, J. C. Stump, have sold to John McCormack one negro woman named Peggy
and her child Lewis, being the same woman sold at sheriffs sale and John Stump
became purchaser in behalf of C. Stump & Co.
C. Stump for C. Stump & Co.   Test: William Smith
Oct. Term 1809 This Bill of Sale was proven in Court by the oath of William
Smith, subscribing witness & ordered to be registered.   [p8]

RAINS, John, Sr.   Bill of Sale   18 Oct. 1809
We, William Gunn, Richard Gunn and Joseph Sumner, of the State of TN, have
sold to John Rains, Senr a negro girl slave named Alse, about fifteen years of
age. Wm Gunn Richard S. Gunn Joseph Sumner
- Oct Term 1809 This Bill of Sale was duly acknowledged in open Court by
William Gunn, Richard S. Gunn & Joseph Sumner and ordered to be registered.
28 Oct. 1809 [p8]

MADDOX, William   Bill of Sale   Dec'r 18, 1809
By virtue of a Power of Attorney given to me by Fielding Lewis of Charles City
County, VA, I have sold a negro man by the name of Frank to William Maddox.
18 Oct. 1809 Thomas E. Waggaman
-Oct Term 1809 The above Bill of Sale was acknowledged in open Court by
Waggaman to be his Act & Deed & ordered to be Registered.   [p9]

BUCHANON, John   Bill of Sale   Dec'r 19, 1809
I, Jessee Westmoreland have sold unto John Buchanon a negro boy slave by the
name of John. 23 Feb. 1808 Jessee Westmoreland
Wit: William Kennedy Moses Ridley
- Oct Term 1809 The above Bill of Sale was acknowledged in open Court by
Westmoreland & ordered to be Registered.   [p9]

SMITH, John H.   Bill of Sale   Dec'r 19, 1809
I, Michael C. Dunn, Sheriff of Davidson County, did on the 14th day of this
month at the Courthouse in Nashville expose in Public Sale to the highest bidder
one negro boy named Ennis; seized as the property of Francis Prince, under an
execution from the County Court of Davidson County at the suit of John Murphy.
At which sale John H. Smith became the purchaser. 16 Feb. 1809
M. C. Dunn, Shff   Test: John Darling
- Oct Term 1809 The above Bill of Sale was duly acknowledged in open Court
& ordered Registered. 28 Oct .1809 [p10]

SMITH, John H.   Bill of Sale   Dec'r 19, 1809
I, Michael C. Dunn, Sheriff of Davidson County, did on the 14th day of this
month at the Courthouse in Nashville expose to public sale to the highest bidder
a negro man called Dick, seized as the property of Francis Prince, under divers
executions from the county Courthouse of Davidson at the suit of the Trustees
of the Cumberland College and Stephen Cambell, Jr & Co. 14 Jan. 1809
M. C. Dunn   Test: John Darling
- Oct Term 1809 This Bill of Sale was duly acknowledged in open Court and
ordered Registered. 28 Oct 1809   [p10/11]

4

POYZER, George   Bill of Sale   Dec'r 19, 1809
I, Bennett Wood, sell to Geo. Poyzee, of Nashville, TN, a certain negro boy slave named Beverly, ten years old. 20 Sept 1809 Bennett Wood
Wit: Jno Waller Henry Hagen
- Oct Term 1809 The above Bill of Sale was proven in open Court by the oaths of John Waller & Henry Hagen & ordered to be Registered. 28 Oct 1809[p11]

POYZER, George   Bill of Sale   Dec'r 19, 1809
I, Robert Hewitt, have sold to George Poyzer a negro boy named John, of the age of sixteen years. 25 Aug 1809 Rob't Hewitt
Wit: Henry Hagen James Marsh
- Oct Term 1809 The above Bill of Sale proven in open Court by the oaths of Henry Hagen & James Marsh & ordered to be registered. 28 Oct 1809 [p12]

TENNISON, Mathew   Bill of Sale   Dec'r 22, 1809
We, William Harding and James Hartgraves, sell to Mathew Tennison one negro man slave, named Dick. The said negro to be Tennisons property until .Harding and Hartgraves pay to said Tennison seventy five dollars.
William Harding James Hartgraves   Wit: John Demoss James Demoss
- Oct Term 1809 The above Bill of Sale with Redemption was duly proven in open Court by the oath of James Demoss and ordered Registered at July Term 1809.   [p12]

HAY, Ann   Release   Dec'r 22, 1809
I, David Hay, one of the heirs of John Hay, dec'd, and entitled to a part of his personal estate, have this day received from Ann Hay, Admx, one gray mare, the property of the estate. And, I do further agree that the admx shall have power to lease and receive the rents of such part of the house and lot in Nashville where Col. William Christmas now keeps his Land Office which I am or may be entitled to as one of the heirs of John Hay, deceased. 12 Nov. 1808
David P. Hay   Wit: B. Searcy
NB I, the above named David Hay, have also this received from Ann Hay, Admx, one Watch and one Saddle. 12 Oct. 1808 David P. Hay
Wit: B. Searcy
- Oct. Term 1809 This Release David P. Hay to Ann Hay, proven in open Court by the oath of Bennet Searcy & ordered to be registered.
28 Oct. 1809   [p13]

HAY, Ann   Release   Dec'r 22, 1809
I, James Campbell, one of the heirs of John Hay, deceased, being entitled to a part of his personal estate as well as real, have this day received of Ann Hay, admx, one bay mare. And I do further agree that the said Ann Hay shall have

power to lease and receive the rents of that part of the House and lot in Nashville where Col. Christmas now keeps his Land Office.
18 Oct. 1809   James Campbell
NB I, the above named James Campbell, have this day received from the said Anny Hay, admx., one Silver Watch being also of the personal estate of the said John Hay, 18 Oct 1809   James Campbell
- Oct. Term 1809 This Instrument of Writing of Release acknowledged in open Court by the said Campbell and ordered Registered. 28 Oct. 1809 [p14]

LEWIS, Wm T.   Bill of Sale   Feb'ry 19, 1810
I, Heydon Wells have sold to William T. Lewis one negro woman slave named Easther, aged twenty five years, and her female child named Kitty, aged one year.
10 Jan 1810 Haydon Wells Wit: J. B. Reynolds, Daniel Collins
- This Bill of Sale was duly acknowledged in open Court by Heydon Wells & ordered Registered 27 Jan 1810 [p15]

CLAIBORNE, Tho. A.   Power of Attorney   Feb'ry 19, 1810
I, William C. C. Claiborne, of the Territory of Orleans, do hereby appoint Thomas A. Claiborne, of the State of Tennessee my True and Lawful Attorney to make a good and sufficient Title to a tract of land containing   acres lying on the waters of Browns Creek in the County of Davidson and State of Tennessee, it being the tract of land on which my family lived , unto William T. Lewis, or to any other person whom he shall appoint, so soon as the consideration money for the same shall be paid.
14 July 1808 William C. C. Claiborne Wit: John Lynd & J. Vassant
- Territory of Orleans, City of New Orleans   Before me, James Mather, Mayor of the City of New Orleans, personally came his Excellency, William C. C. Claiborne, Governor of the Territory aforesaid who did say the foregoing Power of Attorney is his Deed, signed with his true signature in the presence of John Lynd & J. Vassant, Esqrs.   14 July 1808   Jas. Mather, Mayor
    Aug. 24, 1809 Receipt - Received of William T. Lewis $2570.25 in full consideration of the College Tract of Land which William C. C. Claiborne sold to said Lewis. Thos A. Claiborne, Atty in Fact for Wm C. C. Claiborne
- Jan. Sessions 1810 The above receive was duly acknowledged in open Court by Thomas A. Claiborne his Act & Deed.   [p16]

LEWIS, Wm T. & HALL, Charles M.   Security   Feb'ry 19, 1810
I, Samuel Pryor, hereby sell to William Terrell Lewis and Charles M. Hall all the goods & chattles following: thirteen negro slaves: Black Sall, Lucy, Charlotte, Patsy, George, Edmund, Parolee, Charles, Lucy, Ared, Dicy, Yellow Sall & Wyatt; five cows & calves, two steers & twelve head of small cattle; nineteen head of sheep, one hundred head of Hogs, six head of Horses and a

6

Waggon, five beds & their furniture and all my household and kitchen furniture and plate --- Lewis & Hall have this day become Securities for the Stay of a certain execution at the suit of Andrew Jackson & John Hutchings against my property. If the said Samuel Pryor shall pay & discharge the said executions the aforesaid shall be void. June 3, 1809   Sam'l Pryor
Wit: Jno Dickenson, M. C. Dunn
- It is further agreed that if I, the said Pryor, shall remove such goods & chattels from the plantation where I now live, the said Lewis & Hall may take such goods & chattles into their hands & possession.
Jan'y Sessions 1810 This Mortgage Agreement was duly proven in open Court by the oaths of Dickinson & Dunn & ordered to be Registered.
27 Jan 1810 [pp16/17]

POYZER, George   Bill of Sale   February 19, 1810
I, Samuel Hart, of Philadelphia, PA have sold to George Poyzer a certain negro boy slave named Moses, aged twenty six years. 16 Nov. 1809   Sam'l Hart
Wit: Henry Hagan Ilai Metcalf
- January Sessions 1810 The above deed was duly proven in open Court by the oaths of Henry Hagan and Jlai Metcalf & ordered to be Registered.
27 Jan. 1810 [p18]

HERREN, William   Bill of Sale   February 19, 1810
I, William Evans, have sold to William Herren a negro girl named Silvey, eleven years old, for two hundred and twenty five dollars; one hundred and twenty five dollars belongs to Artremineia Herren as a legetee. 21 Oct 1809
William Evans   Wit: Allen Thompson Joseph Hannah
- Jan. Sessions 1810 The above deed was acknowledged in open Court by the said Wm Evans & ordered to be Registered. 27 Jan. 1810 [p19]

BUCHANAN, John   Bill of Sale   Feb'ry 19, 1810
I, Jeremiah Grizzard have sold to John Buchanan a negro man slave by the name of Jim. 8 Jan. 1810 Jeremiah Grizzard   Wit: John Gordon Zachariah Neill
- January Sessions 1810 The above deed was acknowledged in open Court by Jeremiah Grizzard and ordered to be Registered. 27 Jan 1810   [p20]

RIDLEY, George   Bill of Sale   Feb'ry 19, 1810
I, Charles Mulherren, have sold to George Ridley one negro woman named Bet; black mare, one bed and furniture. 27 Jan. 1810 Charles Mulherron
Wit: Sharod Hails James Mulherron
- January Sessions 1810 The above deed was proved in open Court by the oath of James Mulherron and ordered to be Registered 27 Jan. 1810 [p20]

7

LEWIS, Wm T.   Power of Attorney   Feb'ry 20, 1810
I, Peter Bennet, of the County of Knox, and State of TN, do authorize my trusty
friend William T. Lewis to receive all sums of money, certificates or otherwise
that may be coming to me from Major Bennett Craften for his Services as
Second Major in the State Regiment of North Carolina having purchased the
same claim from the heir of Major Bennett Crafton. 16 Dec. 1809 P. Bennet
Wit: Thomas A. Claiborne, J. M. Lewis, Cornelius N. Lewis
- January Sessions 1810 This Power of Attorney was duly proven in open Court
by the Oaths of Thomas A. Claiborne and Cornelius N. Lewis & ordered to be
Registered 27 Jan. 1810   [p21]

SHEPPARD, Henry   Power of Attorney   Feb'ry 20, 1810
I, William Sheppard of the County of Orange in the State of NC, do appoint
Henry Sheppard my attorney to execute a Deed to James Robertson conveying
to him a certain Tract of land, part of a Tract granted to James Robertson and
William Sheppard, being a tract lately purchased of me. Also 640 acres to
Richard Hightower, being a part of a Tract of 5000 acres that was granted to
John Haywood. Also to divide and appropriate the said part of 5000 acres as
allotted to David Moore 300 acres thereof to said Hightower & his 640 acres
and to the heirs of McDowell their 1000 acres and as to the Residue of the said
five thousand acres he is hereby authorized to sell and convey two thousand
acres to any person he may think proper. I authorize the said Henry to settle any
disputes who now exist or are likely to arise by reasons of a certain contract
which I formerly made with Thomas Taylor to convey to him five hundred acres
of land entered in the Western District and near or upon the Mississippi .
15 Aug 1809 Wm Sheppard   Wits: K. Turner   Thomas Haywood
- January Sessions 1810 The above Power of Attorney proved by the oaths of
Kinchen Turner and Thomas Haywood and ordered to be Registered [pp21/22]

DRAKE, Benjamin   Bill of Sale   May 15, 1810
I, Isaac Drake, have sold to Benjamin Drake a certain negro slave, Anthony,
about ten years old. 20 June 1809   Isaac Drake
Wit: William J. Drake   Benjamin Drake
- April Sessions 1810 The above Bill of Sale was duly acknowledged in open
Court by said Isaac to be his act and deed and ordered to be Registered 28 Apr
1810   [pp22/23]

RIDLEY, George   Covenant   May 15, 1810
I, Thomas Hopkins of the County of Sullivan and State of TN, am bound to
George Ridley. The condition of this obligation is thus: George Ridley has sold
his right to a tract of land of 300 acres lying on the South side of Holstein River
apposite the mouth of the N fork of said river. Which tract had been previously

8

purchased by Ridley from William Cocke for which tract a grant was issued to James McNear who afterwards sold the same to David Ross of VA. If the said Hopkins shall save Ridley from all harm and expenses this obligation to be void. Thomas Hopkins   Wits: Thomas Dillon, Bennett Searcy, Robert Searcy
- April Sessions 1810 This Covenant between Hopkins and Ridley proven in Court by the oaths of Bennett Searcy and Robert Searcy. 27 Apr 1810 [p23]

RIDLEY, George   Receipt   May 15, 1810
I have this day received of George Ridley one thousand dollars which is in full for the Bond I have entered into. 14 Apr 1810   Thos Hopkins   Teste: A. Foster
- April Sessions 1810 Receipt duly proven in Court by the oath of Anthony Foster.   [p24]

LEWIS, William T.   Bill of Sale   May 15, 1810
We, Jesse Riggs and Spencer Griffin, have this day sold to William T. Lewis a negro boy slave about fourteen years of age by the name Isaac. 22 Marcy 1801   Jesse Riggs   Spencer Griffin   Test: James Armstrong Joel Riggs
- April Sessions 1810 This Bill of Sale proven in open Court by the oath of Joel Riggs & ordered to be Registered 27 Apr 1810   [p24]

POYZER, George   Bill of Sale   May 15, 1810
We, Thomas and James Ferguson of Nashville, have sold to George Poyzer a negro boy named Dick, about forty two years of age. 29 Jan 1810   Thomas & James Ferguson   Teste: J. R. Bedford   Henry Hagen
- April Sessions 1810 This Bill of Sale proven by the oaths of John R. Bedford & Henry Hagen & ordered to be Registered.   [p25]

JOHNSTON, Oliver   Bill of Sale   May 15, 1810
I, William Scott, Sen'r, have sold to Oliver Johnston three negroe slaves; Prince, Lucinda & her child, Abraham. 16 Feb 1810   William (X) Scott
Test: Finch Scruggs Jas H. Gamble
- April Sessions 1810 The above bill of sale was duly proven by the oaths of Finch Scruggs and James H. Gamble and ordered to be Registered.
27 Apr 1810 [pp25/26]

BURNETT, Leonard   Bill of Sale   May 15, 1810
I, James Mathis have sold to Leonard Burnett one negro woman slave named Cloe, about seventeen years of age and her child, about eleven months old. 22 Jan 1810 James Mathis Test: William Anderson Gab'l Joslin
- April Sessions 1810 The above Bill of Sale acknowledged by James Mathis to be his Act & Deed and ordered to be Registered. 27 April 1810 [p26]

9

CLAIBORNE, Wm F. L.　　　　Bill of Sale　　　　May 15, 1810
I, Thomas A. Claiborne, for the natural love and affection which I entertain for
my son, William F. L. Claiborne as also for his better maintenance, have given
unto my said son, William Ferdinand Leigh Claiborne one Negro woman named
Kizzey, about twenty seven years of age with her increase; Willis, a boy about
five years old; Sally, a girl about three years old; Matilda, a girl about as year
old. 12 Feb. 1810　Thos A. Claiborne　　　　Test: O. B. Hayes, Tho. Crutcher
- April Sessions 1810　The above Bill of Sale duly proven by the oaths of O. B.
Hayes and Thomas Crutcher and ordered to be Registered.
28 April 1810　　[p27]

CLAIBORNE, Mary E. T.　　　　Bill of Sale　　　　May 16, 1810
I, Thomas A. Claiborne, in consideration of the natural love and affection which
I entertain for my daughter, Mary Eliza Tennessee Claiborne as also for her
better maintenance, have given to my daughter a mulatto girl named Rebecca,
about eighteen years of age and her two children, Alfred, a boy about four years
of age & Letitia, a girl about one year old. 12 Feb. 1810　Thos. A. Claiborne
Teste: O. B. Hayes　Thos. Crutcher
- April Sessions 1810　The above Bill of Sale proven in open court by the oaths
of O. B. Hayes and Thomas Crutcher and ordered to be Registered.
28 Apr. 1810　　[p28]

CLAIBORNE, Micajah G. L.　　　　Bill of Sale　　　　May 16, 1810
I, Thomas A. Claiborne, for the natural love and affection which I entertain for
my son, Micajah Green Lewis Claiborne, as also for his better maintenance have
given unto my son Micajah Green Lewis Claiborne a negro woman slave named
Susanna, about twenty years of age with her increase; a boy named Reuben,
about eight years of age and Caswell, a boy about two years of age, also a girl
named Vilate, about eight years old. 12 Feb. 1810　　Thos. A. Claiborne
Test: O. B. Hayes　Thos. Crutcher
- April Sessions 1810　This Bill of Sale was duly proven in open Court by the
oaths of O. B. Hayes and Thomas Crutcher 28 April 1810　[p29]

LEWIS, Mary H., Charlotte F., Maria E., & Peggy　Instrument　May 16, 1810
Whereas I have disposed of certain property which I acquired in right of my
Deceased Wife, Sarah T. Claiborne - to Wit: the plantation called Windsor,
situate near Nashville whereon I lately lived and also Lot #23 in the Town of
Nashville with the buildings and improvements. Whereas a part of the Estate is
intended for my children: William F. L. Claiborne; Mary E. T. Claiborne; and
Micajah G. L. Claiborne. A part of Lot #23 has been sold to William Eastin and
to secure the debt a deed of Trust dated 14 Feb. 1810 was executed. ... among
other things that the money and bonds to be paid my children and their survivors

... that I, Thomas A. Claiborne as well in consideration of the love and affection which I entertain for the Daughters of William T. Lewis; To Wit Mary H. Lewis, Charlotte F. Lewis, Maria E. Lewis and Peggy Lewis do set aside unto them 21Feb. 1810   Thos. A. Claiborne
Teste: O. B. Hayes, Tho. Crutcher, Thomas Eastin
- April Sessions 1810 The above Instrument of Writing duly proven in open Court by the oaths of O. B. Hays & Thomas Eastin and ordered to be Registered. 28 Apr 1810 [pp29/30]

CUMMINGER, Sarah   Deed of Relinquishment   July 18, 1810
I, James Hudgens, for divers good reasons...me moving and more especially to prevent litigation and future compliance with the intention of the will of John Hudgins, my brother, who by his last Will and Testament ... relinquish and renounce for myself and heirs all claim and claims to any part & parcel of the said Estate Bequeathed by the said John Hudgins to Sarah Cumminger.
16 July 1810   James Hudgins   Test: Sam'l Carsson   Thomas Gibson
- July Sessions 1810 This Deed of Relinquishment duly proven by the oaths of Samuel Carson and Thomas Gibson and ordered to be Certified.
17 July 1810 [p31]

EDMONDSON, William   Power of Attorney   July 31, 1810
I, David Buckannon, for divers good causes ... me thereunto moving ... constitute my trusty friend, William Edmondson, my true and lawful attorney to ... secure all such sums of money due and owing to me in this state or any state or territory in the United States of America which may hereafter become due to me ...to transact all my business and affairs as I myself could do ...
26 July 1810 David Buckannan
- July Sessions 1810 This letter of Attorney was duly acknowledged in open Court by said Buchanan and ordered to be Registered. 28 July 1810 [pp31/32]

MARTIN, John   Bill of Sale   August 2, 1810
I have sold to John Martin a negro man slave named George, about twenty years of age. 24 July 1810   Charles Ewing
Test: Phil. Watkins George M. Martin
- July Sessions 1810 The above Bill of Sale was duly proven by the oath of Phillip Watkins and George M. Martin and ordered to be Registered.
28 July 1810   [p32]

HARRISON, Polly   Deed of Gift   August 2, 1810
In consideration of the love & affection I have for my wife, Polly Harrison, I do hereby bequest the following; two beds and their furniture; the household furniture of every kind; one Bay horse & one white cow; likewise the kitchen

11

furniture. 28 August 1807 John Harrison
Test: Jerm Ezell Susannah (X) Ezell
- July Sessions 1810 The above Deed of Gift proved by the oaths of Jerm Ezell
& Susanna Ezell and ordered to be Registered 28th July 1810 [p33]

EWING, Nathan   Bill of Sale   August 2, 1810
I, Betsy Davis, have sold to Nathan Ewing a negro girl slave named Zelpha,
about eight years of age. 23 July 1810 Elizabeth Davis
Test: Will Williams Henry C. Ewin
- July Sessions 1810 the above deed was duly proven by the oaths of William
Williams and Henry C. Ewin & ordered to be Registered. 28 July 1810 [p33]

McCONNEL, John P.   Bill of Sale   August 2, 1810
I, Peter Bennett, of the County of Knox and State of Tennessee, have sold to John
P. McConnell one negro boy by the name of Anthony, about twenty years of age.
11 December 1809 P. Bennett   Test: Wm T. Lewis   Corlis Black
- July Sessions This Bill of Sale was proven by the oaths of Wm T. Lewis and
Corlis Black & ordered to be Registered. 28 July 1810 [p34]

FOSTER, Rob't C.   Bill of Sale   December 4, 1810
I, Stephen Woodston of the County of Goochland and State of VA, have sold to
Robert C. Foster three negro boys ; Warrick, Martin & Spotswood. 4 June
1808 Stephen Woodson Test: John Baird   Smith
- July Sessions This Bill of Sale was proven by the oath of John Baird, one of
the Subscribing Witnesses who also made oath that Smith the other Subscribing
Witness is not now in the State , & ordered to be Registered
28 July 1810 [pp34/35]

SADLER, Mary   Bill of Sale   December 4, 1810
I, Thomas Sadler, have sold to Mary Sadler one negro boy slave named Moses.
29 Sept 1810 Thomas Sadler   Test: Micajah McQuary Jesse Shelton
- October Sessions The above Bill of Sale was duly proven in open Court by
the oaths of Micajah McQuerry and Jesse Shelton and ordered to be Registered.
26 Oct 1810 [p35]

WILEY, Samuel   Bill of Sale   Dec. 4, 1810
I, Joseph Chumbley, did give and bequeath unto Samuel Wiley one Sorrel Mare
four years old her Right Eye Out, also a Sorrel colt one year old next spring, a
star in his forehead. 15 Oct 1810 Joseph (X) Chumbley   Test: Nathan Ewing
- October Sessions This Bill of Sale duly acknowledged to be his act by the said
Joseph Chumbley and ordered to be Registered. 28 Oct 1810 [pp35/36]

12

CURRY, Robert B.   Bill of Sale   Dec. 4, 1810
I have sold to Robert B. Curry a negro girl slave named Kizzy, about sixteen or seventeen years old. 25 Aug 1810   Jas Lewis
Test William Eastin James Wm Lewis   Jno P. McConnell
- October Sessions This Bill of Sale was duly proven by the oaths of William Eastin and James W. Lewis. 26 Oct 1810 [p36]

HAYS, Charles   Bill of Sale   Dec. 7, 1810
I, Gabriel Vest, of the State of Tennessee and the county of Rutherford, have sold to Charles Hays a certain negro man named David, about twenty four years of age. Oct. 1810   Gabriel Vest   Test: Jno H. Smith
- October Sessions This Bill of sale acknowledged in open court by Gabriel Vest & ordered to be registered. 26 Oct 1810 [pp36/37]

DAVIS, John   Bill of Sale   Dec. 7, 1810
I, Joshua Ballance, have sold to John Davis one Brindle Cow and Red Calf, one white cow and white calf, one dark red cow with a white spot and a calf of the same color, one red heifer, one brindle steer; 3 feather beds & furniture and all my household goods with my farming and carpenter tools. 3 Oct 1810
   Joshua Ballance Test: William Greer Abraham Ballance K. P. Wilson
- October Sessions This Bill of Sale proven by the oaths of William Greer and Abraham Balance & ordered to be Registered 25 Oct 1810 [p37]

BINGHAM, Alvan   Contract   15 Dec. 1810
Whereas Eli F. Hill hath invented a new & useful improvement, being a Washing Machine never before known or used in the United States, and whereas by Letters Patent issued under the great Seal of the United States & bearing date the 11 February 1808 ... right of vending to others to use the said machine....Hill has sold unto Selathiel Jackson of Madison County New York , the right to vend to others within the country lying West of the Allegany Mountains ... whereas I, Selathie Bingham , have sold to Alvan Bingham 2nd of the State of Ohio the rights within the States of Tennessee, Kenrucky, those parts of Virginia & Pennsylvania which lie west of the Allegany Mountains, all the Territories west of said mountains & the following Counties in the State of Ohio; Athens, Washington, Muskingum, Belmont, Lucking, Knox, & Tuskarawa. 2 Jan 1810
Salathiel Jackson   Wit: Forrest Meeker
-The Territory of Michigan and of the county of Bourbon in KY and County of Allegany in PA I have sold out of the above mentioned territories and they are hereby excepted. Salathiel Jackson
State of Kentucky   Burban County, the 5th January 1810
This day personally came before me and acknowledged the within to be his hand and deed   Jas Brown   Asst Judge of Burbon Circuit Court

State of Kentucky I, Charles Scott, Governor of the Commonwealth, do hereby certify that James Brown was & still is an assistant Judge for the Burban Circuit Court. 8 Jan 1810 Chs Scott [pp38/39]

Owen, Richard B.   Bill of Sale   7 Feb'y 1811
I, Real Grigg have sold to Richard B. Owen two negro slaves, one a man called Jerry, the other a girl called Anny. 12 July 1810 Real Grigg Wit: J. Whiteside Sam'l Jackson
- - The condition of the above Bill of Sale ... Real Grigg would have Rich'd B. Owen to stand surety for him in a Bond to Bennet Blackman ... if Grigg pays, said Bill of Sale to be void. [p39]
-January Sessions 1811 The above Bill of Sale between Grigg and Owen proved in open Court by the oath of Felix Grundy, who says he is well acquainted with the hand and believes the signature J. Whiteside to his proper hand writing and that he is now in the City of Washington. Nathan Ewing says he believe it is the handwriting of Jenkin Whiteside and that he believes he is at this Federal City, ordered Bill of Sale be registered. 1 Feb. 1811 [p40]

CURRY, Robert B.   Bill of Sale   20 Feb. 1811
I, John Hawkins, have sold to Robert B. Curry one negro boy slave named Beverly, about twelve years old. 27 Nov. 1810 John Hawkins Wit: B. J. Bradford Isaiah Curry
-January Sessions The above bill of sale duly acknowledged by said Hawkins and ordered to be Registered. 2 Feb. 1811 [p40]

HOOPER, Joseph   Bill of Sale   20 February 1811
I, James Terrell have sold to Joseph Hooper a negro woman and two children by the names of Janey, Harry and Isaac. 30 Oct 1810 James Terrill
Wit: Benj'm Branch Celia L. Moore
- Jan. Sessions The above Bill of Sale was acknowledged by Terrill to be his Act & Deed & ordered to be Registered. 2 Feb. 1811 [p41]

BELL, George & Rob't   Bill of Sale   20 Feb'ry 1811
We, Susannah Pryor, Admx, Benjamin Pryor and John Barnard have sold to George and Robert Bell the following negroe slaves; a negro man named Wyatt, a woman called Charlotte, one by the name of Lucy, one by the name of Sally, one boy called George and a girl called Patsy, being six in number. The above negroes are sold by consent of the legatees to discharge a debt to Jackson and Hutchings. 26 January 1811
Susannah Pryor, Admx   Benj'm W. Pryor   John Bernard
Wit: Jos Coleman Peter J. Voorhies
- Jan. Sessions The above Bill of Sale was duly proven in open Court by the

14

oath of Joseph Coleman, one of the subscribing witnesses. 2 Feb 1811 [pp41/42]

MOORE, David   Bill of Sale   21 Feb'ry 1811
I, William Renucks, of the County of Madison in the Mississippi Territory have sold to David Moore, Doctr of Phisic of the County of Davidson in the State of Tennessee a certain negro boy slave named Isham. Said Renucks shall be released from the payment of fifty dollars on the 1st day of March 1812 if said Renick shall repurchase said negro. 2 Feb. 1811   William Renick
Test: William Edmondson J. Haywood
- Jan. Sessions The above Bill of Sale was duly acknowledged in Open Court by the said William Renicks & ordered to be Registered. 2 Feb. 1811 [pp42/43]

FITZHUGH, Samuel   Bill of Sale   21 Feb'ry 1811
I, John Edmonds, have sold certain property to Samuel Fitzhugh; one negro man slave named James, one by the name of Tom, one woman named Neaton and one by the name of Junar and her two children, Joseph and Edmond; a boy by the name of Peter; Together with all my household furniture and Stock of Horses, Cattle and Hoggs. Nevertheless the said Samuel binds himself to relinquish his claim to said property whenever I relieve him of certain debts wherein he is my security. 31 Oct. 1810 John (X) Edmonds
Test: N. Gatlin James (X) Fitzhugh
- Jan. Sessions This Bill of Sale was duly proven in Open Court by the oaths of Nathan Gatlin and James Fitzhugh and ordered to be Registered 2 Feb. 1811 [P43]

BOYD, Richard   Bill of Sale   21 Feb'ry 1811
I, William L. Boyd, have sold to Richard Boyd three negro slaves; Fanny, aged about twenty four years, and her two children, Alfred, five years of age and his sister, Zeny, about six weeks of age. 7 Feb. 1810. This is to be fully understood, the above named negroes was formerly the property of Francis Prince and afterwards the property of Drury Forde which was morgaged to me by Drury Ford and by the request of Ford I have sold them for the named sum. W. L. Boyd
-Jan Sessions The above Bill of Sale was duly acknowledged in Open Court by the said William L. Boyd to be his Act and Deed and ordered to be Registered. 2 Feb 1811 [p44]

McNAIRY, Jno & LYTLE, Wm   Bill of Sale   21 February 1811
I, Robert Renfro, have sold to John McNairy and William Lytle, Jr. the following household and kitchen furniture; six featherbeds & furniture, one walnut cupboard & furniture, eight walnut tables, three dozen chairs, six Dutch ovens, one eight gallon pot, two frying pans, one skillet, two tea kittles, six water pails,

one candlestand, two brass candlesticks, one large waiter, three pairs of andirons, two trunks all other articles he is now possessed of. Whereas the said McNairy & Lytle, have become Security for the said Robert Renfro and are bound to Jenkin Whiteside, Esquire for the payment. If payment and interest are made the above deed shall be void. Robert (X) Renfro Wit: Robt Searcy - Jan. Sessions The above Bill of Sale was proven in Open Court by the oath of Robert Searcy and ordered to be registered. 2 Jan 1811 [pp44/45]

POYZER, George   Bill of Sale   21 February 1811
William Gunn of Bedford County, Tennessee has sold to George Poyzer a negro woman slave named Sylvia, about the age of forty years. 8 April 1809
Wm Gunn   Wit: Jlai Metcalf D. Robertson
- Jan. Sessions The above Bill of Sale was proven by the oath of Duncan Robertson, one of the Subscribing Witnesses and ordered to be Registered. 2 Feb. 1811 [p46]

FOSTER, Robert C.   Bill of Sale   21 Feb. 1811
I, Stephen Woodson of the State of Virginia, have sold to Robert C. Foster of Tennessee three negroe slaves; a man named Warrick, his wife named Cate and their youngest child, a girl named Cloe. 15 Feb 1809   Stephen Woodson
        Wit: Wm Maddox   E. S. Hall
-Jan. Sessions This Bill of Sale was duly proven in open Court by the oath of Elihu H. Hall, one of the Subscribing Witnesses, and also that the other witness, William Maddox is Dead. Ellis Maddox being duly sworn says the signature 'Wm Maddox' is the proper handwriting to the best of his knowledge and belief. Ordered the same be registered. 2 Feb 1811 [pp46/47]

BREIFF, Jas, LORD, Jno., & TALBOT, Thos.   Bill of Sale   15 March 1811
I, Whythe Sym, have sold to James Brieff, John Lord & Thomas Talbot a negro woman slave named Polly and her increase to administer the profits to the sole and separate use of Jane Wheaton of the town of Nashville, without the interference of her husband, Calvin Wheaton. 19 May 1807 Wythe Sym
Test: I. A. Parker Sophia Talbot
-March Term This Bill of Sale was proven by the oath of Isham A. Parker, one of the Subscribing witnesses and ordered to be Registered. 13 March 1811 [pp47/48]

WHEATON, Calvin   Bill of Sale   15 March 1811
I, Samuel Elliott have sold to Calvin Wheaton a negro woman named Becky, about twenty six years of age and her three children, Polly, Daniel & Philley.
20 May 1809   Samuel Elliott
Calvin Wheaton has this day become Security for Samuel Elliott in a suit in the Superior Court of Mero District in which Unity Mennan is plaintiff and Samuel

Elliott & wife, defendants. If Elliott shall indemnify himself this bill of sale to be void. Samuel Elliott Test: Tho Hickman J. Wharton

-March Term This Bill of Sale was proven in open court by the oaths of Thomas Hickman and Jesse Wharton and ordered to be registered 13 March 1811 [p48]

CAFFREY, Mary   Bill of Sale
          23 March 1811

I, William D. Anderson have sold unto Mary Caffrey, widow of John Caffrey of the county of Claiborne, Mississippi territory, one negro man slave, named Levin, whom I bought at the sherrifs sale in an execution against dec'd in favour of Banlong Felts on the 8th Nov. 1806. W. D. Anderson
Test: Alex'r Ewing, John Hoggatt

- This Bill of Sale was proven in open court by the oaths of John Hoggatt & ordered to be registered. 23 March 1811 [p49]

COX, John & COX, James H.   Bill of Sale   2 April 1811

I, Archiles Cox, for the love and affection I bear and have to my children, John Cox and James H. Cox, do convey to my two sons the following property, two negro girl slaves, one named Mourning, about fourteen years of age; the other named Aggy, about seven years of age, and their increase, and also two horse beasts, a roan mare and colt, two feather beds and furniture, a cow and calf and my stock of hogs to have share & share alike. 14 Nov 1810   Archiles Cox
Test: Ric'd Garrett, Hugh Norvell, Jesse Fly, Wm Bulmer, Thos. Rutherford

-Jan. Term This Bill of Sale proven in open Court by the said Archiles Cox and ordered to be Registered. 29 Jan 1811 [pp49/50]

POYZER, George   Instrument   2 April 1811

Whereas Eli F. Hill, a citizen of the United States, hath invented a new and useful improvement, being a washing machine ... patent issued under the Seal of the United States, dated 11 Feb. 1809 ... Hill has conveyed unto Salathiel Jackson of the State of New York, the right to use the machine within the large and extensive country lying west of the Allegany Mountain ... sold to Alvan Bingham of the town of Athens, Ohio the right to vend in the State of Tennessee have sold to Geo Poyzer the aforesaid right to vind within the county of Davidson for a term of fourteen years. 14 Dec. 1810. Alvan Bingham third
Test: Th. Hill, Charles Cassidy, Henry Gros, Henry Hagan.

The following are the names of single rights sold before .me: James McBride, James Buchanan, David C. Snow, Oliver Johnson, George M. Deaderick, Wm Betts, Sr., Betts, Jr, Chapman   Alvan Bingham third
Test: Th. Hill, Charles Cassidy, Henry Gros, Henry Hagan

-Jan Sessions Above Instrument proven in Open Court by the oaths of Henry Gros and Henry Hagan & ordered to be Registered. 29 Jan 1811 [pp50/51]

SANDERS, Francis   Bill of Sale   10 May 1811
I, Kintchen Freeman, have sold to Francis Sanders a negro boy slave by the name
of Harry, about seven years of age. 23 March 1811   Kintchen Freeman
Test: John Moore, Goodspeed S. Stokes
-April Sessions - the above Bill of Sale was proven in Open Court by the oaths
of John Moore and Kintchen Freeman and ordered to be registered. [p51]

Ballows, Thos. G.   Bill of Sale   10 May 1811
I, Jeremiah Sullivan, have sold to Thomas G. Ballow eighteen head of Hoggs,
two feather beds and furniture, one side saddle and trunk and loom, six chairs,
cotton wheel, one dish, 12 plates, 6 knives, coffee pot, 6 cups and 6 saucers. 29
Jan 1811   Jeremiah (X) Sullivan
Wit: David Pulley, Zachariah Sullivan & James B. Moore
- April Term This Bill of Sale was duly proven by the oaths of David Pully and
James B. Moore and ordered Registered. [p51/52]

JAMES, Joshua   Bill of Sale   7 Aug 1811
I, Johnston Vaughn, have sold to Joshua Jones a negro girl named Hannah slave,
about sixteen years old. 14 Feb 1811   Johnston Vaughn
Test: John Harding, Elijah James, G. West
- July Sessions 1811 The above deed duly proven by the oaths of John Harding
and Elyah James and ordered to be Registered. [p52]

TALBOT, Clayton   Bill of Sale   10 Aug 1811
I, Edmond Gregary, have sold to Clayton Talbot one negro woman, named Edy,
about thirty five years of age, one negro boy named Simon, about fourteen years
of age and one other negro boy named Fortune, about ten or eleven years of age.
15 April 1811 Edmond Gregary   Test: Eli Talbot, Wm Rickard
- July Sessions This Bill of Sale acknowledged in Open Court by Edmond
Gregory and ordered to be Registered. [p53]

HARDING, John   Bill of Sale   10 August 1811
I, John C. Bradshaw, have sold to John Harding a negro woman Betty and her
two children, Letty & Anja. Betty about twenty one years of age, Letty about two
and a half years old and Anja about nine months. 11 July 1811
John C. Bradshaw   Wit: William Griffin
- July Sessions The above Bill of Sale acknowledged in Open Court by John C.
Bradshaw and ordered to be Registered. [p53]

STRINGFELLOW, Robert   Bill of Sale   10 August 1811
I, Elizabeth McDonald, have sold to Robert Stringfellow a certain negro woman
named Dinah, about twenty one years old. 23 Feb. 1811

Elizabeth (X) McDonald Wit: Jonathan Johnston, Alexander Wm McDonald
- July Sessions The above Bill of Sale proven by the oath of Jonathan Johnston
and Alexander Wm McDonald and ordered to be Registered. [p54]

WHITESIDE, Jenken   Bill of Sale   10 August 1811
I, Richard Apperson, Mechlinbvurg County, VA, have sold to Jenkens Whiteside
three negro slaves; Pleasant, a man, Cate, his wife and her youngest child, Lacky.
22 June 1811 R. Apperson
Test: John Read, Willis R. Smith, O. B. Hayes
- July Sessions The above Bill of Sale proven by the oaths of John Read and O.
B. Hayes and ordered Registered. [p54]

ELLISTON, Joseph T.   Bill of Sale   13 Aug 1811
We, Joseph Scales and John Nichols, have sold to Elliston a certain negro man
slave named Prynus, about twenty eight years of age. 5 June 1811   Jos Scales
& Nichols & Co.   Test: Thos. Shackelford, Robert Elliston
-July Sessions The above Bill of Sale proven by the oath of Thomas
Shackleford and Robert Elliston and ordered Registered. [p55]

OVERTON, John   Bill of Sale   13 August 1811
I, Elihu S. Hall, have sold to John Overton one negro man slave named
Abraham, aged eighteen years. 22 March 1811 E. S. Hall   Test: J. Wharton
- July Sessions The above bill acknowledged in open court by the said El.ihu
S. Hall and ordered Registered. [pp55/56]

CATO, Green   Bill of Sale   14 August 1811
I, Roland Cato., Senr, give to my beloved son Green Cato, my negro boy
George, about three years old. 22 July 1811 Roland (X) Cato
Test: John Stump, Lewis Earthman
- July Sessions The above Bill of Sale acknowledged in open Court by the said
Roland Cato to his Act & Deed and ordered to be Registered. [p56]

CATO, Roland, Junr   Bill of Sale   14 August 1811
I, Roland Cato, Senr, give to my beloved son Roland Cato, Junr, my negro boy
Peter, the son of my negro woman Philis, aged about four years of age. 22 July
1811 Roland (X) Cato   Test: John Stump, Lewis Earthman
- July Sessions The above Bill of Sale acknowledged in open court by the said
Roland Cato to be his act and deed and ordered to be Registered. [p56]

JACKSON, Sam'l & RAYMOND, N. Order of Redemption   14 Aug. 1811
I, James Terrell, have sold to Samuel Jackson and Nicholas Raymond a certain
stud horse named 'Duke of Bedford', another stud horse called 'Lviather', and

19

one bay gelding called 'Doctor', also five feather beds and furniture, two hundred head of hoggs, twelve head of cattle ... whereas we have become bound as Securities for a bond signed also by Ephraim Parham, payable 18 months after its date to Joseph Kerr, Robert Gardner, Joseph Sawyers, and Samuel Lambeth. The intention of the above is alone to secure the said Samuel and Nicholas ... otherwise the same is to totally null and void. 20 July 1811
James Terrell   Test: John E. Beck
- July Sessions the above Redemption was acknowledged in open court by the said James Terrell and ordered to be Registered. [p57]

JOSLIN, James   Bill of Sale   14 August 1811
I, Daniel Joslin, have sold unto James Joslin one negro girl slave ten or eleven years old. 4 March 1811 Daniel (X) Joslin
Test: George Wade, Fre. Mothershed
- July Sessions Bill of Sale proven in open Court by the oath of George Wade, one of the subscribing witnesses and ordered to be Registered. [pp57/58]

CRICHLOW, Henry   Bill of Sale   14 August 1811
I, Augustine Jones, have sold to Henry Crichlow a certain negro woman slave named. 22 July 1811   Augustine Jones   Test: John Alford Wm F. Brodnax
- July Sessions This Bill of Sale was acknowledged in Open Court by the said Jones and ordered Registered [p58]

HAYES, Oliver B.   Bill of Sale   14 August 1811
I have sold to O. B. Hayes a negro boy named Patrick, aged thirteen years.
23 Oct. 1810. Wm W. Kavanaugh   Test: Felix Grundy Andrew Jackson
- July Sessions   This Bill of Sale was proven in Open Court by the oaths of Felix Grundy and Andrew Jackson and ordered Registered. [p58]

TUNSTALL, Geo. B., Peyton H. & Edm. S.   Bill of Sale   16 August 1811
I, Edmund Tunstall, have for the love and affection which I bare to my three youngest sons; George Brook Tunstall, Peyton Henry Tunstall and Edmund Savage Tunstall, given the following negroes; Telus, Celia, Jude, York, Solomon, Marcus and Rody, together with their increase ... further convey to my said children all my household and kitchen furniture and all my stock of horses, except my mare, 'Meretrix', 'Virginia Nole Melangere & Sir Harry Teazell, as also one wagon and gear. 30 Nov 1810 Edm. Tunstall
Test: B. J. Bradford Jas Tunstall Wm McQuiston
- July Sessions This Bill of Sale proven by the oaths of Benjamin J. Bradford and James Tunstall & ordered to be Registered. [p59]

TUNSTALL, Ruth Anne   Bill of Sale   16 August 1811
I, Edmund Stall, have in consideration of the love and affection which I have
unto my Dear Daughter, Ruth Anne Tunstall, given her a negro girl named
Milley and her increase. 30 Nov 1810   Edm. Tunstall
Test: B. J. Bradford   Jas Tunstall Wm McQuiston
- July Sessions The above Bill of Sale proven in Open Court by the oath of
Benjamin J. Bradford and James Tunstall and ordered Registered. [p59]

WYAND, Henry   Deed of Gift   16 Sept 1811
I, Henry Wyand, for the love and affection I bear to my children; John Wyand,
Daniel Oldemburg Wyand, Catherine Wyand and Jacob Wyand, given the
following property: a negro girl slave Ciorna, one carriage and horse, three beds,
bedsteads and furniture and one bureau and book case, one carpet, two sets of
window hangings, one dozen of chairs and one table. 11 July 1811
Henry Wyand   Test: Phil. Watkins, B. D. Rutherford, - B. Soread?
- Sept. Term Davidson County Circuit Court The above Deed of Gift was
proven in open Court by the oaths of Benjamin D. Rutherford and Burwell
Soriad? and ordered to be Registered. [p60]

PARHAM, Ephraim M.   Indenture   30 Sept. 1811
This Indenture made 13 April 1811 between James and Edmund Terrell (so far
as relates to the Stud Horse bya the name of the 'Duke of Bedford', and James
Terrell alone as to the other property of the one part and Ephraim M. Parham of
the other part.. .... agreeable to two judgments which Tabitha Wilkins recovered
against Edmond Terrell before John Goodrich, J.P., on 27 March 1811 ... doth
hereby sell the following property: one Stud Horse called by the name of the
'Duke of Bedford,' also a negro man named Jack, one Stud colt called
'Dungannon', two Stud work horses both named 'Dick; and a large roan mare,
one grey mare, one sorrel mare with a blaze face, purchased of Hooper, one
small black mare, and nine colts now in the pasture of Jacob Dickinson. The
above property to be conveyed to said Parham until he is fully discharged.
James Terrill Edm'd Terrill   Test: Wllis Martin J. R. Motheans? Robert
Adams
-April Sessions 1811 The above Indenture acknowledged by the said James
Terrill and ordered to be Registered. [p60/61]

BASS, Laurence   Indenture   18 Sept 1811
John S. Williamson doth sell to Laurence Bass two negro slaves, one a male
named David, about twenty two years old; the other a female named Suekey,
about 28 years old if said John S. should fail to pay the debt which he owes to
Laurence as Administrator of John Patton , deceased. If said debt of $818.62 is
paid with interest before the first day of January next he will release said

agreement. 18 Sept 1811 John S. Williamson Laurence Bass
Test: J. Whiteside Clem Hall
-Sept. Term Davidson Circuit Court This Deed of Trust was acknowledged by
John S. Williamson and Laurence Bass and ordered Registered. [p62]

HOGGATT, John   Bill of Sale   18 Nov. 1811
I, Aaron Owens of Sumner County, have sold to John Hoggatt one negro girl
slave named Grace. 6 March 1811   Aaron Owens
Test: M. C. Dunn Thos Shackleford
- Oct. Sessions This Bill of Sale proven in Open Court by the oaths of Michael
C. Dunn and Thomas Shackleford and ordered Registered. [p63]

EWING, Alexander   Bill of Sale   3 Dec. 1811
I, William R. Bell, have sold to Alexander Ewing four negroes; George, a negro
man about thirty years of age; his wife Sarah and their two children, Peggy &
Mary, the oldest about four years old and the youngest about nine months. 10
Dec. 1811   W. R. Bell Test: Geo. Bell, Hugh F. Bell
-Oct. Sessions 1811 This Bill of Sale was acknowledge by W. R. Bell and
ordered to be Registered. [p63]

EWING, Alexander   Bill of Sale   3 Dec. 1811
I, James Dupree, have sold to Alexander Ewing a negro woman slave named
Milley, about twenty years of age. 13 Sept 1811   Jas. Dupree Test: Rich'd
Rassier John Frazar
-Oct. Sessions This Bill of sale proven by the oaths of Richard Rapier and John
Frazier and ordered to be Registered. [p64]

BARROWS, Mathew   Bill of Sale   3 Dec. 1811
I. Edmond Gregory, have sold unto Mathew Barrow a negro boy slave by the
name of Anthony, about fifteen years of age. 6 June 1811 Edmond Gregory
Test: Joshua Meuborn Littleton Johnson
p Oct. Sessions This Bill of sale proven by the oath of Littleton Johnson and
ordered to be Registered. [p64]

COCKE, John W.   Bill of Sale   3 Dec. 1811
I, William Purnell, have sold to John W. Cocke one negro fellow named William
and one negro girl named Frankey. If John W. shall pay his debt this Bill of Sale
to be void. 22 Oct 1811 Wm Purnell   Test: John E. Beck Benj'm Joslin
- Oct. Sessions This Bill of Sale acknowledged by said William and ordered to
be Registered. [p65]

MENEES, James   Bill of Sale   4 Dec. 1811
This day sold to James Menees a certain negro girl slave named Aggy, about
fourteen years of age. 21 Oct 1811
Martha Turner, Admx of James Turner, deceased
Test: Thos. Kirkman Clem Hall
-Oct Sessions This Bill of Sale proven in open Court by the oaths of Thomas
Kirkman and Clem Hall and ordered Registered. [p65]

LEVY, William   Deed of Gift   14 Dec. 1811
I, Henry Levy, do give unto my son, William Levy, all my stock of horses, cattle
& hogs; also all my household furniture and also my crops and all the remainder
of my property I do give and Bequeath to my son William Levy.   Henry Levy
    Test: Robert Lucas William Lucas Thomas (X) Levy
- Oct Sessions This Deed of Gift was proven in open Court by the Oath of
Robert Lucas and William Lucas and ordered Registered. [p66]

WILSON, Dan'l and John   Deed of Trust   14 Dec. 1811
I, Nancy Wilson do transfer to Daniel and John Wilson for and in consideration
of my maintenance and the maintenance of my six children during our lives, all
my interest and upon the consent and agreement of my husband all his right, title
and interest to that property which to us has been devised by the Last Will and
Testament of our Fathers, James and Thomas Wilson. 21 Oct 1811
    Nancy (X) Wilson   Test: Jno Overton Tho Overton
- Oct Sessions This Deed of Trust was acknowledged by the said Nancy Wilson
to be her act and deed and ordered Registered. [pp66/67]

BURLAND, Thomas M.   Bill of Sale   13 Feb'ry 1812
I have sold to Thomas M. Burland a negro girl slave named Betty. 9 March
1811 James Anderson   Test: Was. L. Hannum John Cockrill
- Jan Sessions This Bill of Sale proven by the oath of Washington L. Hannum
and John Cockrill and ordered Registered. [p67]

HOOPER, Joseph   Bill of Sale   13 Feb'ry 1812
We have sold to Joseph Hooper a negro man named Jack, which James Terrill
purchased of Rich'd Baskervill. 19 Nov 1811
James Terrell Ephraim M. Parham   Test James W. Exum
- Jan. Sessions This Bill of Sale was proven by the oath of James W. Exum and
ordered Registered. [p67]

HOOSER, Wm   Bill of Sale   13 Feb'ry 1812
I, Charles Hays, have sold to William Hooser one negro man named Peter, about
the age of twenty two years. 3 Sept 1810 Charles Hayes

Test: Robert Edmondson
- Jan. Sessions Bill of Sale acknowledged by Charles Hays and ordered Registered. [p68]

BURLAND, Thomas M.   Bill of Sale   13 February 1812
I, Edmond Gregory, have sold to Thomas M. Burland a negro slave man named Dick, about forty years old or thereabout and also Harry, about nineteen years old. 20 April 1811 Edmond Gregory   Test: Geo. Poyzer
- Jan. Sessions This Bill of Sale proved by the oath of George Poyzer and ordered Registered. [p68]

CRUTCHER, Thomas   Bill of Sale   13 February 1812
I, Thomas Napier, have sold to Thomas Crutcher a negro boy named Ezekiel; it being for payment of an execution in the hands of M. C. Dunn, Sheriff, against me. 19 April 1809 Thos Napier   Test: M. C. Dunn
- Jan. Sessions This Bill of Sale proved by the oath of Michael C. Dunn and ordered Registered. [p69]

HODGE, James   Bill of Sale   13 February 1812
I, John Edmonds, have sold to James Hodge one negro boy named Peter, going on eight years old. 13 July 1811   John (X) Edmons
Test: Edley Ewing Thomas Williamson
- Jan. Sessions This Bill of Sale was proved by the Oath of Edley Ewing and ordered to be Registered. [p69]

HALL, Elihu S.   Bill of Sale   13 February 1812
This Indenture between Michael C. Dunn, Esqr & Sheriff of Davidson County, and Elihu S. Hall. Whereas on 29 April 1811 a writ was issued out of the Court of Pleas and Quarter Sessions of Davidson County a certain Josiah Horton and Richard Boyd against Judith Ford and Polly Pendleton, heirs of Francis Prince, deceased ...against debts of Francis Prince ... levied upon a negro slave named Judy ... said Sheriff did expose to public sale said slave named Judy and Elihu S. Hall became the highest bidder. 12 August 1811
M. C. Dunn, Shff of Davidson County   Test: Wm H. Bedford Henry Hagan
-Jan. Sessions This Bill of Sale was acknowledged by M. C. Dunn and ordered Registered. [p70/71]

PARHAM, Ephraim M.   Bill of Sale   14 February 1812
I have sold to Ephraim M. Parham four horses. 19 Nov 1811 Joseph Hooper
Test: James W. Exum
- Jan. Sessions This Bill of sale proved in open Court by the oath of James W. Exum & ordered Registered. [p71]

24

MASTERSON, Thomas   Bill of Sale   14 Feb'ry 1812
I, James Curtis, have sold to Thomas Masterson three negro slaves; Judy, a woman of the age of thirty seven, Nancy a child of Judy's about six years of age and Allen, also a child of said Judy, about four years of age. If I pay my debt to Thomas Masterson this Bill of Sale to be void. 22 Jan. 1812 Jas. Curtis
Test: E. Pritchett Stephen Cantrell, Jnr
- Jan. Sessions This Bill of Sale with Redemption was proven by the oath of E. Pritchell and Stephen Cantrell Junr and ordered Registered. [p72]

BURLAND, Thomas M.   Bill of Sale   14 Feb'ry 1812
I have sold Capt. Thomas M. Burland a certain negro woman slave named Rachel, about thirty five years old, yellow complexion. 19 March 1811
William Eastin
- Jan. Sessions This Bill of Sale acknowledged by Eastin and ordered to be Registered. [p73]

BURLAND, Thomas M.   Bill of Sale   15 February 1812
We, Nichol and Ramsey, have sold to Thos M. Burland a negro boy named Jack, about seven years old. 17 April 1811   Nichol & Ramsey
- Jan. Sessions This Bill of Sale acknowledged in Open Court by Thomas Ramsey for Nichol and Ramsey and ordered Registered. [p73]

PORTER, Alexander   Bill of Sale   15 Feb'ry 1812
I, Henry Jones, (Boatsman) have this day sold to Alexander Porter a Barge or Boat known by the name of 'Cumberland Snow' now on the River Cumberland at Nashville... if debt is paid this deed to be null and void. 26 Nov. 1811 H. Jones   Test: D. Moore Jno Baird
-Jan. Sessions This Bill of Sale with Redemption was proven in Court by the oath of David Moore and John Baird and ordered Registered. [p74]

MAXWELL, Jesse   Bill of Sale   17 Feb. 1812
We, Thomas Williamson, William Ramsey and Edley Ewing have sold to Jesse Maxwell two negro slaves; Jim and Neaton. 20 Jan. 1812 Thomas Williamson
Wm Ramsey Edley Ewing   Test: John Alford, James Hodge
- Jan. Sessions This Bill of Sale was acknowledged by the oath of James Hodge and ordered Registered. [p74]

VEST, Gabriel   Bill of Sale   17 February 1812
I, James Jackson have sold to Gabriel Vest a Negro girl named Kitty, about 17 years old both healthy & sound except her present illness from having had a child about eight days ago and since dead. I agree to keep her until she can be safely removed. John Jackson for James Jackson

25

Test: Bennet Blackman, William Eastin
- Jan. Sessions the above Bill of Sale acknowledged in open court by the said James Jackson and ordered to be Registered. [p75]

RAMSEY, William   Bill of Sale   17 February 1812
I, John Edmonds, have sold a negro man slave named Tom, Joe and Edmond, boys, and all my houshold furniture, hogs, horses and stock of every kind. John (X) Edmonds   Test: Thomas Williamson
- January Sessions This Bill of Sale was proven in open Court by the oath of Thomas Williamson and ordered to be Registered. [p75]

SAUNDERS, Edward   Bill of Sale   17 Feb 1812
We, Edmund Cooper and John Camp have sold to Edward Saunders one negro slave man by the name of James of a *molataish* complection this 23rd day of Jan. 1812. Edm'd Cooper   Jno Camp
- January Sessions The above Bill of Sale was acknowledged in open Court by the said Cooper and Camp and ordered to be registered. [p76]

NELLY, Granny   Bill of Sale   17 February 1812
I, William Lytle Bledsoe of Sumner County, have sold to *Granny Nelly one man of colour said to be her son, by the name of Daniel Turner. 5 Dec. 1811
          W. L. Bledsoe   Test: Robert B. Curry, Jas. G. Read
- January Sessions The above Bill of Sale was proven in open Court by the oath of Robert B. Curry and James G. Read and ordered to be Registered. [p76]

BOYD, Wm L.   Bill of Sale   17 February 1812
This Indenture made this fifth day of December 1809 between Drury Ford of Montgomery County and William L. Boyd of Davidson County. Drury Ford has sold the following negro slaves; a negro woman named Fanny, aged twenty three; and her two children named Alfred, about five, and one three weeks of the name Leny. William L. Boyd has become security of Francis Prince in an appeal from the Court of Pleas for Davidson County to the Superior Court of Law for the District of Mero wherein Joseph Wharton was plaintiff and said Francis was defendant. If the above shall be paid with interest the above indenture to be of no effect. Drury Ford   Wit: John Lemaster
- January Sessions The above Bill of Sale with Redemption was proven in open Court by the oath of John Lemaster and ordered Registered. [pp77/78]

ELLISTON, Joseph T.   Bill of Sale   3 March 1812
I, James Merry of the county of Charlotte and state of Virginia, have sold to Joseph T. Elliston a negro man named Isaac, about forty three years of age. 9 Nov. 1811   James Merry by Prettyman Merry his Atty in fact

Test: Robert Elliston, James Young

- January Sessions This Bill of Sale was proven in open Court by the oath of James Young and also says he believes that Robert Elliston is now a resident of the state of KY. [pp78/79]

EWING, Nathan   Bill of Sale   3 March 1812
I, John Newman, have sold to Nathan Ewing a negro boy slave named Flanders, about fifteen years of age. 31 Jan. 1812   J. Newman   Test: Jasper Sutton, Henry C. Ewin
-Jan. Sessions The above Bill of Sale proven by the oaths of Jasper Sutton and Henry C. Ewin and ordered to be Registered. [p79]

BOSWORTH, William   Bill of Sale   March 9, 1812
I have sold to William Bosworth a negro girl, Judy and Child. Jan. 4, 1812
    John Marr   Test: Duncan Robertson
- January Sessions The above Bill of Sale was acknowledged in open Court by John Marr and ordered to be Registered. [pp79/80]

STUMP, Frederick   Bill of Sale   May 8th 1812
I, Christopher Stump, have sold to Frederick Stump a negro man by the name of Peter. C. Stump by Lin. T. Turner   Test: Jno. C. Hall, Jno. Frazer
- April Sessions This Bill of Sale acknowledged in Court by Lemuel T. Turner, attorney, and ordered to be Registered. [p80]

GOODRICH, John   Bill of Sale   May 8, 1812
I have sold to John Goodrich two negro boys; Lewis and Ned this 29 Nov 1811. Willis Maclin Wit: Edmond Goodrich, Thomas Camp, Jno. Beck, Howel Harris
    - April Sessions The above Bill of Sale proven by the oaths of Edmond Goodrich and John Beck and ordered to be Registered. [p80]

LANIER, Arrabella   Bill of Sale   May 8, 1812
I, Isaac Lanier, of Stuart County, TN, have given unto my Daughter, Arrabella, nine negro slaves: Dick, a negro man about forty years; his wife, Lucy about forty seven years old and her son Peter, about eleven, and her daughter Easter, about eight years old, and her daughter, Hannah about six years old and her daughter, Delse, about four years old and a boy named Nero, about seventeen years old and a boy named Cantra about 18 years old and a girl named Mary, about eleven. The above named Arrabella is not to call on named Isaac Lanier, nor his heirs for any property received, either before or hereafter from Col. John Sampson or from Col. Richard Clinton, Deceased. Should she or her Representatives now or hereafter claim any part of the aforesaid Estates the above obligation to be void. J. Lanier

27

Test W. R. Bell, Patsy Bell, Elizabeth (X) House, George Heginty
- April Sessions 1812 The above Bill of Sale proven by the oath of William R.
Bell and George Haginty and ordered to be Registered. [pp81]

HARWOOD, John R. Bill of Sale May 8, 1812
I have sold to John R. Harwood a negro girl slave named Milly. 21 April 1812
Thomas Ridley
- April Sessions The above Bill of Sale was acknowledged in open Court by the
said Thomas Ridley and ordered to be Registered. [p82]

RIDLEY, Moses Bill of Sale May 8, 1812
I have sold to Moses Ridley five negroes; one man named Martin, one woman
named Nance and one girl named Nance and a boy named Cheseman and a boy
named Charles. 31 March 1812 John R. Harwood
Test: William Lain, Alex'r M. Harwood
- April Sessions This Bill of Sale proved in open Court by John R. Harwood.
[p82]

RIDLEY, Thomas Bill of Sale May 8, 1812
I have sold to Thomas Ridley five negroes; one man named Berryman, one
woman named Lairy, one boy named York, one boy named Bradock and a girl
named Abb. 1 March 1812 John R. Harwood
- April Sessions The above Bill of Sale was acknowledged by the said John R.
Harwood and ordered to be Registered. [pp82/83]

HARMON, Richard D. Bill of Sale May 9, 1812
I, Willie Barrow, have sold to Richard D. Harmon four negroe slaves; one
woman aged about twenty one years and her child Susannah, and two girls aged
about fifteen years, one named Mary, the other, Nutter. 17 March 1812 W.
Barrow
- April Sessions The above Bill of Sale acknowledged by Willie Barrow to be
his Deed and ordered to be Registered. [p83]

SAUNDERS, Francis Bill of Sale May 9, 1812
I, Jas. Coleman, have sold to Francis Saunders a certain negro man named John.
15 February 1812 Jas Coleman Test: Jno. Summerville, Jno. Anderson
- April Sessions The above Bill of Sale was proven by the oath of John
Summerville and John Anderson and ordered to be Registered. [p83]

HALL, Elihu S. Bill of Sale May 9, 1812
Whereas a Writ dated 3rd Monday in Oct., 1811 was issued at the Instance of
Howel Tatum against Henry H. Edwards ... was levied on a negro woman slave

named Joanna and her child, Eliza, and it was advertised according to Law that Joannah and Eliza would be sold to the highest bidder on the 23rd of Nov. at the Courthouse in the Town of Nashville and Elihu S. Hall was the purchaser. Therefore I, Michael C. Dunn, Sheriff of Davidson County convey to the said Elihu S. Hall before mentioned negroes; Joannah. about eighteen years of age and her child Eliza about eighteen months old. 23 Nov. 1811 M. C. Dunn
- April Sessions The above Bill of Sale was ackrowledged in open Court by Dunn and ordered to be Registered. [p84]

COCKRILL, John, Senr & COCKRILL, Mark Bill of Sale   May 9, 1812
I have sold to John Cockrill, Senior and Mark Cockrill the following property; one negro slave woman named Rachel, about forty years old; one negro woman named Bed, about twenty years old; one negro boy named Jack, about six years old; one negro man named Dick, about forty years; one negro man named Harry, about forty years old; one negro man, also named Harry, about twenty five years old; two large bay horses purchased of Drury Pullam; one bay horse purchased of Mr. Garner; one sorrell mare which he got from John Nickols; one horse called Buck which he received as a gift from John Cockrill; one small white horse, called Poney, purchased from the said John Cockrill; one dun horse purchased in Kentucky; bay mare purchased of Mr. Holland and one bay Stud received as a gift from John Cockrill; one bay mare called ribbon purchased from Cockrill; one roan more purchased from Mark Cockrill; one sorrell mare and a three year old colt which he received from John Cockrill; one bed, bedstead and furniture, sideboard purchased of Mr. Deatherage and one Secretary, one Bureau, one Cupboard, Six Chairs, and firefender, two tables, one Waggon and gear, three shot guns, four cows and two yearling cattle, one gigg, two candlesticks, forty yards of blue and black cloth. 15 Feb. 1812   Thos. M. Burland Test: Joseph Green, Was. L. Hannum
- April Sessions The above Bill of Sale was acknowledged in open Court by Thomas M. Burland and ordered to be Registered. [p85]

SMITH, John H.   Bill of Sale   May 9, 1812
Rec'd of John H. Smith one hundred and fifty dollars, the amount of cash I advanced Thomas Kirkman on 19th of December last for her claim to one negro child named Essie, about six years old. I release all my claim to her this 25th December 1811   McKernan and Stout   Test: G... W. Martin
- April Sessions The above Bill of Sale Burnard McKernan and Samuel V. D. Stout was acknowledged by them and ordered to be Registered. [p86]

ELLISTON, Joseph T.   Bill of Sale   May 9, 1812
I, Roger B. Sappington, have sold to Joseph T. Elliston a certain negro man named Jerry, about twenty eight or nine years old. 5 March 1812

Test: Thos. Hickman, James Connelly, Robert Elliston
- April Sessions The above deed proved in open Court by the oaths of James Connelly and Robert Elliston and ordered Registered. [p86]

SMITH, John H.　　　　Bill of Sale　　　　May 9, 1812
I have sold to John H. Smith a negro slave boy named Drury Filler, aged about twelve years. Nath Wyche　　　Test: Joseph Park
- April Sessions The above Bill of Sale acknowledged in open Court by Nathaniel Wyche as his Deed and ordered to be Registered. [p87]

FELTS, Cary　　　Articles of Agreement　　　　May 9, 1812
Cary Felts does lend to Lewis Allen and his wife two negroes by the name of Sam and one negro girl by the name of Rhody, one horse by the name of Snip and one feather bed. Said Allen does not have any right or title to the above named property more than the use and labour of said property and that Felts is to pay the taxes of said property. 12 Jan 1812　Lewis Allen
Test: Joseph Burnett, Christopher F. Felts
- April Sessions The above Article of Agreement proven in open Court by the oaths of Joseph Burnett and Christopher F. Felts and ordered to be Registered. [p87]

CURRY, Robert B.　　　Bill of Sale　　　　May 9, 1812
I, Churchill Anderson, of King & Queen County and State of Virginia by my Attorney in Fact, William Cox of the County & State aforesaid, have sold to Robert B. Curry a negro man named Humphrey, about twenty years old. 18 March 1812　William Cox　Test: John Gwin, Wm Lientz
- April Sessions The above Bill of Sale was proven by the oaths of John Gwin and William Lientz and ordered to be Registered. [p88]

JOHNSTON, Oliver　　　Bill of Sale　　　　May 9, 1812
I, William Nash, late of Montgomery County and State of Pennsylvania, have sold to Oliver Johnston the following negro slaves; Solomon, about twenty one years old; James, about sixteen years old; Jenny, about ten years old; David, about seven; and Jefferson, about four or five years old. Said slaves were lately the property of John Evans, deceased and by him devised to said William Nash. 23 March 1812
William Nash by his Attorney in Fact Andrew Gelkeson　　　Wm Nash
Test: R. McGavock, Jno L. Ewing , William Philips, Elisha Williams
- April Sessions 1812 The above Bill of Sale proven by the oaths of William Philips and Elisha Williams and by Randal McGavock and John L. Ewing and ordered to be Registered. [pp88/89]

WHITESIDE, Jinkin   Bill of Sale   June 25, 1812

I, Thomas Dillon, have sold to Jinkin Whiteside eight negro slaves; one female slave named Chaney, about thirty four years old and her seven children; John, Cain, Davy, Henry, Lucy, Elvira and Elsey. If debt is paid this Bill of Sale to be void. 13 Marcy 1812   Thomas Dillon

- Third Circuit Smith County I, Robert Allen, Clerk of said Circuit Court of Smith County do hereby certify that the above Bill of Sale was acknowledged in open Court by Thomas Dillon and ordered to be Registered. 2 April 1812 Robert Allen, Clk [pp89/90]

WHITESIDE, Jinkin   Bill of Sale   August 7, 1812

I, Charles B. Neilson, have sold to Jinkin Whiteside a certain negro slave named Abby, about twenty years of age ... Whiteside has paid to Charles B. for which a negro boy, Offey, was mortgaged by Doctor A. Whiteside to the late firm of Neilson, King and Mitchell of Franklin of which William King of Abingdon was a partner and William Trigg surviving Executor of the last Will etc. of said William King, deceased claims for the same money. If said Neilson shall pay debt this deed to be void. 18 July 1812 C. B. Neilson
Test: Robt Searcy, J. R. Bedford

- July Sessions Bill of Sale with Redemption proven in open court by the oath of Robert Searcy and John R. Bedford and ordered to be registered. [p91]

TAIT, Wm   Bill of Sale   August 7, 1812

I, Robert Stothart, have sold to William Tait the following negro slaves: Tom, a negro fellow about thirty five years old; Geary, a negro fellow about twenty three years old; Daniel, a negro fellow twenty five years old; David a negro fellow about seventeen years old; Henry, a negro boy about fourteen years old; Adam, a negro boy about twelve years old and Richard a negro boy about eleven years old; Mary, a negro woman about thirty five years old and her child about six months old; Also my undiv'd half of four negro women and one negro man in possession of William and George Newell in the Mississippi Territory. 20 Feb. 1812 Rob. Stothart   Test: David Tait, Lewis Sturdivant

- July Sessions The above Bill of Sale acknowledged in Open Court by the said Robert Stothart and ordered to be Registered. [p92]

TAIT, Wm   Bill of Sale   7 Aug. 1812

I, Rob. Stothart, have sold the following negro slaves; Olivey, a negro woman about thirty six years, Charlott, her daughter, fifteen years of age; Willis, her brother, eleven years old and Rachael, a negro girl of sixteen years old. 14 Nov. 1811   Robt Stothart Test: David Tait, Lewis Sturdivant

- July Sessions The above Bill of Sale was acknowledged by the said Robert Stothart and ordered to be Registered. [pp92/93]

CREEL, Wm   Bill of Sale   7 Aug 1812
I, Elijah Dotson, have sold to William Creel a negro woman named Charlotte,
about twenty two years old. 11 May 1812   Elijah Dotson
Test: William B. Dotson
 - July Sessions The above Bill of Sale acknowledged in open court by the said
Elijah Dotson and ordered to be Registered. [p93]

NICHOLS, John   Bill of Sale   7 Aug 1812
I have sold to John Nichols a certain negro woman by the name of Hannah, about
twenty five years of age. 22 Feb. 1812   James Hudgens
Test: R. Weakley, Joseph Scales
 - July Sessions The above Bill of Sale acknowledged in open Court by the said
James Hudgins and ordered to be Registered. [p94]

GWATHNEY, John B.   Bill of Sale   7 Aug 1812
I, William Bean, have sold to John B. Gwathney a negro woman named Dorcas
aged twenty and two negro children; the eldest a girl aged four years, named
Maria; the second a boy two years old named Frederick. 22 July 1812
William Bean   Test: Sto. D. Hays
 - July Sessions   The above Bill of Sale proven in open court by the oath of
Stockley D. Hays and ordered Registered. [p94]

DILLAHUNTY, Thomas   Bill of Sale   9 Aug 1812
I, John Dillahunty, Senr, for the love and affection I have for my son Thomas
Dillahunty, do give him one negro boy slave named Stephen, about six years old.
11 July 1812   John Dillahunty
Test: Joel Anderson, Silas Dillahunty, Nathan Williams
 - July Sessions The above Bill of Sale proven in open Court by the oath of Joel
Anderson and Silas Dillahunty and ordered Registered. [pp94/95]

COCKE, Jno. W. to PURNELL, Wm   Instrument of Writing 7 Aug 1812
Release of a Bill of Sale with Redemption, registered in this book on page 65...
July 21, 1812 Received with interest in full discharge of said mortgage.
 J. W. Cocke
 - July Sessions The above Instrument acknowledged in open court by Cocke
and ordered Registered. [p95]

WEAKLEY, Robert   Bill of Sale   7 Aug 1812
I, James B. Risque, have sold to Robert Weakley the following negro slaves:
Pamely, Charlton, Rosilla, Edmond, Garland, Polly, Maria, Letticia and Susan.
29 April 1811 James B. Risque   Test: William Quarles, Benj. P. Howard
 July Sessions The above Bill of Sale proven in open Court by the oath of

William Quarles and ordered to be Registered. ...witness also made oath at Benjamin P. Howard is not an inhabitant of this state as he believes. [p96]

CLAIBORNE, Thos. & COOKE, Wm W.   Bill of Sale   7 Aug 1812
I, John Baylor Gwathney, have sold to Thomas Claiborne and William W. Cooke seven negro slaves; Lewis, Phil, Jacob, Carter, Dorcas and her two children, Maria and Frederick.   Christopher Stump has commenced a suit against Gwathney and Thomas Claiborne and William W. Cooke hath become the appearance bail and if Gwathney truly make his personal appearance at the October Sessions this sale to be void. 5 July 1812   J. B. Gwathney
Test: S. D. Hays, Wm L. Butler
 - July Sessions This Bill of Sale with Redemption proven by the oaths of Stockley D. Hays and William L. Butler and ordered Registered. [pp96/97]

EWING, Nathan   Bill of Sale   7 Aug 1812
I, John Jones of Stuart County, TN, have sold to Nathan Ewing a negro man slave named Fed, about thirty one years of age. 10 March 1812 John Jones
Test: Andrew Casselman, J. B. Neville, H. C. Ewing
 - July Sessions The above Bill of Sale proved by the oath of Andrew Casselman and Henry C. Ewing and ordered Registered. [pp97/99]

BOYD, Richard   Bill of Sale   7 Aug 1812
I, Benjamin Dunn, have sold to Richard Boyd one negro woman by the name of Mason, nineteen years of age. 27 Nov. 1811 Benj. Dunn
Test: G. Whitson, John Smith
 - July Sessions The above Bill of Sale proved by the oath of George Whitson, one of the subscribing witnesses, who also made oath that John Smith is not as he believes an inhabitant of this state, and ordered Registered. [p98]

WHALEN, Mary Magdalen & her two children   Deed of Gift   18 Nov 1812
I, Frederick Fisher, in consideration of the good will and affection I bear towards Mary Magdalen Whalen and two of her daughters, Elizabeth Whalen and Cathrina Whalen, I do constitute them to be my true and lawful heirs of all my Real and Personal Estate. 14 Oct 1812   Frederick Fisher
Test: John Brooks, Mathew Brooks
 - October Sessions This Deed of Gift acknowledged in open Court by the said Frederick Fisher and ordered Registered. [p99]

BOYD, Richard   Bill of Sale   18 Nov 1812
I, William Roper, have sold to Richard Boyd one negro boy slave by the name of John, about thirteen years of age of a complexion with a remarkable white place on the left side of his forehead. 10 Oct 1812

William Roper   Test: M. C. Dunn, C. Hewitt
- October Sessions This Bill of Sale was proven by the oaths of Michael C. Dunn and Caleb Hewitt and ordered Registered. [pp99/100]

GLASS, Sinai   Deed of Gift   18 Nov 1812
I, Peggy Glass, in consideration of the natural love I have for my daughter, Sinai Glass, and also for the better maintenance of her hath given to her, my legal heir, all my Real and Personal Estate; one Bed and furniture, one furniture Chest, one trunk, one side saddle, one big wheel and one pair of cards, five chairs, one dozen plates, five bowls, six tin cups, one coffee pott, two dishes, one set knives and forks, one stue kittle, one frying pan, two tin kittles, one sifter and one table. 23 Oct 1812 Peggy (X) Glass   Test: C. Stump, Philip Shute
- October Sessions This Deed of Gift was acknowledged in open court by Peggy Glass and ordered Registered. [p100]

GOODIN, Sarah WRIGHT, Betsy BLAN, Arthur Deed of Gift 19 Nov 1812
I, Arthur Blan, in consideration of the natural love I bear unto my beloved Daughters, Sarah Goodin & Betsy Wright and my beloved son, Arthur Blan, give unto Sarah Goodin one negro girl slave about two years old named Thankful & two head of sheep and one heifer And to my daughter Betsy Wright one negro girl about four years old named Alley and etc And to my son, one negro man named Stephen, about thirty five years old, one negro woman named Beck about twenty nine years old; one negro boy named Eli, about ten years old; one negro boy named Nathan about eight years old; one negro boy named Isaac about four years old; two cows and calves, two heifers and one sorrell filly, ten head of sheep, twenty head of hoggs and three feather beds and four coverlids, one pot and oven, three ploughs and two weeding hoes. 24 Aug 1812
     Arther {X) Blan   Test: Elsey Roach, Benajah Gray
- October Sessions This Deed of Gift was acknowledged by the said Arther Blan and ordered Registered. [pp100/101]

BLAIR, John   Bill of Sale   19 Nov 1812
I, Nimrod Hooper, have sold to John Blair one negro woman slave named Hager, about twenty years old. 24 Oct 1812 Nimrod Hooper   Test: Benj. Josten
- October Sessions This Bill of Sale was acknowledged by Nimrod Hooper in open Court and ordered Registered. [p101]

WEAKLEY, Robert   Bill of Sale   19 Nov 1812
I, Edward Cage of Bedford County, TN, have sold to Robert Weakley a negro man of a black complection about twenty three years old by the name of Luke; also a negro woman, nineteen, by the name of Rose, also black, and wife of Luke. 21 July 1812   Edw'd Cage   Test: Joseph B. Porter, Will Bradshaw

- October Sessions This Bill of Sale proved by the oaths of Joseph B. Porter and William Bradshaw and ordered Registered. [p102]

HOMES, William   Bill of Sale   23 Nov 1812
I, Richard D. Harman, have sold to William Homes a certain negro girl slave named Mary, aged eighteen. 24 Aug 1812   Richard D. Harman
Test: Lewis Earthman, John Gentry
- October Sessions This Bill of Sale acknowledged by the said Harmon and ordered to be Registered. [pp102/103]

YARBROUGH, Edmund & Jas.   Deed of Gift   23 Nov 1812
I, Jones Read, in consideration of affection I have for James Yarbrough, Jr. & Edmund Yarbrough give and bequeath unto them two feather beds and furniture now in possession of James Yarbrough, Senr; also one cotton wheel, one dutch oven, one skillet with the balance of the household furniture. 22 Oct 1812
    Jones Read   Test:
- October Sessions This Deed of Gift was acknowledged in open Court by Jones Read and ordered Registered. [p103]

TAIT, William   Bill of Sale   23 Nov 1812
We have sold to William Tait a negro boy slave named Ben, or Benjamin, thirteen years of age. 22 Oct 1812 Benjamin Standley   Sam'l Goode
Test: N.A. McNairy, Wm B. Robertson
- October Sessions This Bill of Sale acknowledged in open Court by the said Benjamin and Samuel and ordered Registered. [pp103/104

NICHOL, John   Bill of Sale   24 Nov 1812
We, Nichol & Shaifer, merchants of the Town of Gallatin, Sumner County, TN, have sold to John Nichol, Merchant of Nashville, a certain negro boy named Anderson, about thirteen years of age. 20 July 1812
  Nichol & Shaifer by Abraham K. Shaifer, Acting Partner
Test: R. Armstrong, Peter A. Young
- October Sessions This Bill of Sale proved by the oaths of Robert Armstrong and Peter A. Young and ordered Registered. [p104]

ELLISTON, Joseph T.   Bill of Sale   24 Nov 1812
I, Hugh Dunlap of the county of Roan and State of Tennessee have sold to Joseph Ellison a certain negro man slave named Enoch, about thirty two years of age. 15 Sept 1812 Hugh Dunlap by John Kenelsey, atty
Test: Robert Elliston, John Elliston
- October Sessions This Bill of Sale proven by the oath of Robert Elliston and ordered Registered. [p105]

35

VEST, Betsy   Bill of Sale   24 Nov 1812
We, Nancy and Polly Vest, hereby convey to Betsy Vest all our title vested in us by a Bill of Sale from Gabrial Vest to us his children for a negro boy named Joe, about nine years last April. 15 Sept 1812 Nancy Vest Polly Vest
 Test: John Buchanan, S. J. Ridley
 - October Sessions This Bill of Sale was proven by the oath of John Buchanan and ordered Registered. [p105]

BARROW, Mathew   Bill of Sale   8 Feb. 1813
I, Duncan Robertson, have sold to Mathew Barrow a negro girl slave by the name of Franky, aged fifteen years; now in the possession of George Martin, and the property of Joel Rice, Madison County M. T. 20 Jan. 1813
Duncan Robertson Test: Robert Elliston, John Elliston
 -Jan. Sessions This Bill of Sale probed by the oath of Robert Elliston and John Elliston and ordered Registered. [p106]

BECK, John E.   Bill of Sale   10 Feb. 1813
I, William B. Robertson, sell to John E. Beck a negro girl named Teeny. 29 January 1813. Wm B. Robertson
 -January Sessions This Bill of Sale acknowledged by William B. Robertson to be his act and deed and ordered Registered. [p106]

ELLISTON, Joseph T.   Bill of Sale   10 Feb. 1813
I, Edward D. Hobbs, have sold to Joseph T. Elliston a certain negro boy, named Peter, about twelve years old. 4 Dec. 1812 Edward D. Hobbs
Test: Wm Thompson
 - January Sessions This Bill of Sale acknowledged by the said Edward D. Hobbs and ordered Registered. [p107]

BENOIT, Earnest   Bill of Sale   10 Feb. 1813
I, William Young, have sold a negro man named Nace, twenty one years old, to Earnest Benoit this 25th day of January 1813. William Young
Test: Geo Poyzer
 - January Session This Bill of Sale acknowledged by William Young and ordered Registered. [p107]

CLEMONS, James   Bill of Sale   10 Feb. 1813
I, George Scott, sell a negro woman slave named Jane to James Clemons. 2 Nov. 1811 George Scott Joshua Abston Test: James Douglass, Isaac Clemons
 - This Bill of Sale George Scott and Joshua Abston to James Clemons was acknowledged by the said Scott and Mary Abston for Joshua Abston, dec'd, late her husband, and ordered to be Registered. [p108]

TERRELL, Jas COCKE, Jno W. & WHITE, Wm Bill of Sale   10 Feb. 1813
This Indenture to secure the punctual payment of a a balance due to John W.
Cocke. James Terrell does sell to William White a negro man named Daniel.
If said James Terrell does pay the remainder of the debt this deed to be void.
Originally executed by Samuel Jackson to Thomas Harwood . 19 October 1812
    James Terrell, J. W. Cocke, Wm White
  Test: Wythe Syms, N. G. Childress
  - January Sessions This Indenture of Bargain & Sale with Redemption proven
by the oath of Wythe Syms and ordered to be Registered. [pp108-110]

CAMPBELL, Michael   Bill of Sale   27 March 1813
I, Robert Gillespie of the County of Seneca & State of New York, having
received patent, bearing date 2 April 1810, of a new and useful improvement in
the art of distilling, being a still of oblong form ... have sold to Michael
Campbell of the county of Davidson the right of constructing and vending in the
county of Davidson and State of Tennessee. 6 April 1811   R. Gillespie
Test: Jno. P. McConnell, Wm E. Kennedy, Jas. Porter
  - Jan. Sessions The above transfer of the patent right of a new way of distilling
proven by the oaths of James Porter and William E. Kennedy and ordered
Recorded. [p110/111]

WINN, Louisana   Bill of Sale   22 May 1815
I have sold to Louisana Winn, daughter of Richard Winn, deceased, a negro girl
named Sally, about seven or eight years old. 14 November 1812   Thomas
Crutcher
  - April Sessions This Bill of Sale acknowledged by Thomas Crutcher and
ordered Registered. [pp111/112]

TOLBOT, Sophia W.   Bill of Sale   22 May 1813
I, James Curtis, have sold to Sophia W. Tolbot one negro girl slave named
Nancy, about seven or eight years old. 2 December 1812   Jas. Curtis   Test:
Tho. Crutcher, H. C. Ewin
  - April Sessions This Bill of Sale proven by the oaths of Thomas Crutcher and
Henry C. Ewin [pp112/113]

MENIFEE, James N.   Bill of Sale   22 May 1813
I, Earnest Bernoit, have sold to James N. Menifee a negro man by the name of
Ned, aged twenty. 5 April 1813   Ernest Benoit   Test: Duncan Robertson
  - April Sessions The above Bill of Sale acknowledged by Benoit and ordered
Registered. [p113]

DOUGLASS, William   Bill of Sale   22 May 1813
I, Michael Gleaves, have sold to William Douglass a negro boy named Harry,
aged fifteen. 2 Feb. 1813   Michael Gleaves
Test: Francis McKay, James (X) Castilow
 - April Session The above Bill of Sale acknowledged by Michael Gleaves to be
his act and deed and ordered Registered. [p114]

EDMONDSON, William   Bill of Sale   22 May 1813
I have sold to Wm Edmondson two negro girls, named Anna and Tabby.
26 Feb. 1813   William C. Tucker
Test: Wm Howlet, Geo. Ridley, J. N. Menefee
 - April Session   The above Bill of Sale proven by the oaths of William
Howlet and. James N. Menifee and ordered Registered. [p115]

SAPPINGTON, Roger B. Bill of Sale   22 May 1813
I, Edwin Hickman, have sold to Roger B. Sappington a negro man slave by the
name of Abraham. 11 Feb. 1813   Edwin Hickman
Test: Jacob McGavock, Henry Philips
 - April Sessions The above Bill of Sale acknowledged by Edwin Hickman and
ordered to be recorded. [p116]

BARROW, Matthew   Bill of Sale   22 May 1813
I, John P. Hickman of the town of Huntsville, have sold to Matthew Barrow a
negro girl slave by the name of Franky, aged about fifteen years. 30 March 1813
Jno. P. Hickman Test: Tho. Childress, E. H. Foster
 - April Sessions The above Bill of Sale proven by the oath of Thomas Childress
and Ephrain H. Foster ordered to be registered. [p117]

SAPPINGTON, Roger   Bill of Sale   6 September 1813
I, Jos. T. Elliston, have sold Roger B. Sappington a negro man named Jerry,
which said negro I bought of said Sappoington and do transfer all right & title.
30 December 1812   J. T. Elliston   Test: Will Lytle, Rich. B. Owen
 - July Sessions - the above Bill of Sale acknowledged by Joseph T. Elliston and
ordered registered. [p118]

SAPPINGTON, Roger B.   Bill of Sale   6 September 1813
I, Rees Porter, of Giles County and State of Tennessee, have sold to Roger B.
Sappington a negro man slave by the name of Jerry. 11 December 1811   Rees
Porter   Test: Joseph B. Porter, J. C. Smith
 - July Sessions The above Bill of Sale was proven by the oath of Jacob C.
Smith and ordered Recorded. [p119]

BOYD, George W.   Bill of Sale   8 September 1813
I, Terrence Byrns, have sold to George W. Boyd one wagon and team, consisting
of four horses. 3 Dec. 1812   Torrence Burns   Test: B. J. Braxton,
 - July Sessions This Bill of Sale was proven by the oath of Benjamin J.
Bradford and ordered Registered. [p119]

IRWIN, David   Bill of Sale   9 September 1813
Whereas Joel Rice obtained an Execution against Benjamin J. Bradford and
Edmond Tunstall at April Session 1813 , levied by me on two negro slaves,
Jenny, about thirty five years and Pink, about fifteen, and having advertised ... on
17 July 1813 I sold said negro girl Pink to David Irwin.
19 July 1813   Caleb Hewitt, Dpt Sheriff   Test: John Wright
 - July Sessions This Bill of Sale acknowledged by Caleb Hewitt and ordered
Registered. [p120]

CALDWELL, Joseph   Bill of Sale   20 October 1813
I, James Hodge, convey to Joseph Caldwell all my title and interest in a certain
quantity of negroes; Chloe and her increase, that were willed to my mother in
law, Dorcas Becton by her father Sam'l Slade of North Carolina during her
lifetime and at her death to be equally divided amongst her children living at her
death, to which I'm entitled to a share being one of the heirs. Chloe and increase
are in the State of Georgia; taken there by Sam'l Slade Becton who is entitled to
one seventh part of the whole estate. 20 July 1813
     James Hodge   Test: Philip Pipkin, John Johns
 - October Sessions The above Bill of sale proven by the oath of Philip Pipkin
and ordered to be Registered. [p121]

CALDWELL, Joseph   Bill of Sale   20 October 1813
I, Asa Becton, convey to Joseph Caldwell all my title and interest I have to
negroes in the State of Georgia which belonged to my grandfather and given to
my mother her lifetime and then to her living children; Chloe and her increase
in Georgia, taken there by my brother, Samuel Slade Becton, which said Samuel
is entitled to a seventh of the whole. 19 July 1813   Asa Becton
Test: J. T. Elliston, Joseph McBride
 - October Sessions The above Bill of Sale proven by the oath of Joseph T.
Elliston and ordered to be Registered. [p122]

CALDWELL, Joseph   Bill of Sale   20 October 1813
I, Thomas Dillahunty, do convey to Joseph Caldwell all my title and interest to
a certain parcel of negroe slaves; Chloe and her increase, that was willed to my
mother in law, Dorcas Becton by her father, Sam'l Slade of N. Carolina during
her lifetime and at her death to be divided amongst her children living at her

death to which I am entitled to a share. Chloe and increase are in the State of Georga and were taken there by Sam'l Slade Becton, who is entitled to one seventh share. 8 October 1813   Tho. Dillahunty   Test: Wm Mullin

- October Sessions The above Bill of Sale was proven by the oath of William Mullin and ordered to be Registered. [p123]

GLEAVES, Michael   Bill of Sale   23 October 1813
I, Thomas Taylor, have sold to Michael Gleaves a certain negro boy named Harry, fifteen years old. 1 February 1813   Thos. Taylor
Test: Francis McKay, Thomas Taylor

- October Sessions This Bill of Sale acknowledged by said Taylor and ordered to be Registered. [p124]

McLEMORE, John C.   Bill of Sale   28 October 1813
I have sold John C. McLemore a negro woman of yellow complexion, named Mima, of the age of twenty years. 12 Oct. 1813   James Read
Test: Isaac Settles, James Vaule

- October Sessions This Bill of Sale proven by the Oaths of Isaac Settles and James Vaule and ordered Registered. [p125]

WHITESIDES, Jenkin   Bill of Sale   20 December 1813
We, David and Washington Perkins, have sold to Jenkin Whitesides two patent stills, containing about one hundred and ninety gallons each; one ditto containing about one hundred and eighty gallons, one containg about one hundred and twenty gallons and two other stills; one of about one hundred and thirty gallons, the other about eighty gallons, and about two hundred still tubs for mashing etc; being all the stills and tubbs in and about the Distillery of D. & W. Perkins near Haysborough. David and Washington Perkins are indebted to Whitesides and if they pay said debt the above deed shall be void. 29 April 1813
    David Perkins   Washington Perkins   Test:
- November Sessions The above Bill of Sale was acknowledged by David and Washington Perkins and ordered to be Registered. [pp126/127]

BUTLER, John S.   Bill of Sale   24 January 1814
I, James Carter, sell to John S. Butler one negro boy named Abreham, about sixteen years old. January 12, 1814   James Carter   Test:
- January Sessions This Bill of Sale was acknowledged by the said James Carter and ordered Registered. [p128]

SEAT, William P.   Bill of Sale   24 January 1814
I, Brooking Burnett, have sold to William P. Seat a negro boy named Tom. 11 Oct 1811 Brooking Burnett   Test: John B. Seat, Lemuel Lawrence

- January Sessions This Bill of Sale was proven by the oaths of Lemuel Lawrence and John B. Seat and ordered Registered. [p129

SPRIGGS, Robert   Bill of Sale   24 January 1814
I hereby sell a negro man slave named Ferry, aged nineteen years.
 11 November 1813 Rob't B. Mitrchell   Test: James Jackson
- January Sessions This Bill of Sale proven by the oath of James Jackson and ordered Registered. [p130]

SHUTE, John   Bill of Sale 16 February 1814
I, Robert W. Hart, have sold to John Shute a negro man, Charles, aged about twenty three years; a negro woman, Suckey, aged about thirteen; Henry, about six; Charlotty, about four years of age. 12 Nov. 1813
   R. W. Hart   Test: James Trimble, Jn B. Craighead
- January Sessions This Bill of Sale was proven by the oath of James Trimble and John B. Craighead. [p131]

WARD & PARTON   Bill of Sale 16 February 1814
I, Joseph Watkins, have sold to Ward and Parton one negro boy named Ishmuel.
11 April 1811 Joseph Watkins Test: B. McKiernan, James McCombs
- January Sessions This Bill of Sale proven by oaths of Bernard McKiernan and James McCombs and ordered Registered. [p132]

BROWN, Henry   Bill of Sale   16 Feb 1814
I, John Harwood, have sold to Henry Brown the following negroes with their present increase and any they may have: Simon; Dolly and child, Hanes, Chaney and James. 13 March 1813. John Harwood
Wit: Jared McConnica, Littleton Brown
- This Bill of Sale was proven by the oaths of Jared McConnico and Littleton Brown and ordered Registered. [pp132/133]

ERWIN, Joseph   Bill of Sale   16 Feb. 1814
I, John Shute, have sold to Joseph Erwin a negro man Charles, aged about twenty three; negro woman named Suckey, aged about thirteen; Henry, about six years; Charlotty, about four years. 30 Dec. 1813 John Shute
Test: James Trimble, John Erwin
- This Bill of Sale was proven by the oath of James Trimble and John Erwin and ordered Registered. [p133]

McLEMORE, John C.   Bill of Sale   16 Feb. 1814
I, John Armstrong of the County of Warren and State of Tennessee, have sold to John McLemore of the town of Nashville one negro boy named Moses, seven

years of age sometime in April next. 18 Dec. 1813

John Armstrong   Test: Tho. Childress, Stewart Cowan
- This Bill of Sale was proven by the oath of Thomas Childress and Stewart Cowan and ordered Registered. [p134]

BARROW, Willie   Bill of Sale   7 March 1814
On 22 January 1812 an execution was issued by the County Court of Davidson County by William Guinn, plaintiff against John W. Clay and came in my hands as sheriff of said county; said execution levied upon a negro woman named Rose, a negro girl named Ansy, a negro child named Rose, a negro girl named Polly and a negro girl named Maria. On 17 February 1812 at the Courthouse in Nashville Willie Barrow became highest bidder. I, Michael C. Dunn as sheriff, do hereby sell said negroes. 26 October 1813
M. C. Dunn, Sheriff of Davidson County Test: G. G. Washington, H. P. Bass
- This Bill of Sale acknowledged by Michael C. Dunn and ordered Registered. [p135]

KINGSLEY, Alpha   Mortgage   16 May 1814
I, Joseph Coleman, do sell to Alpha Kingsley the following negroes: Rachel, Ussa, Muria, Kitty, Alfred, Charles, Charlotte, Hannah, Amy, Jiney and Lewis, to secure a debt. If said debt is paid with interest the said sale shall be void. 13 July 1813   Jas. Coleman Test: Jno. Anderson
- This Deed of Mortgage was acknowledged by Joseph Coleman and ordered Registered. [p136]

KINGSLEY, Alpha   Mortgage   16 May 1814
I, Joseph Coleman, sell to Alpha Kingsley the following property; four sections of land in Madison County on the waters of the Hurricane Fork of Indian Creek and also part of two lots of ground on College Hill below the white house on said hill and adjoining the lot said house stand. Kingsley has endorsed a note to M. C. Dunn . If Coleman pay and discharge said debt the above to be void. 13 October 1813   Jas. Coleman   Witness: James S. Brown, Peter Alexander
- This Deed of Mortgage was acknowledged by Joseph Coleman and ordered Registered. [p137]

HOGGOTT, John   Bill of Sale   16 May 1814
Abraham Sandifur of Wilson County, on 14 December 1807, did convey four negro slaves; Stephen, now about forty two years of age; Dick, about thirty five; old Judith, about fifty years of age, and her daughter, Judith, about eighteen years of age to a certain John Lancaster in trust to secure payment to John Haggott. Standifur stands justly indebted to Hoggott and does sell said four slaves and their increase to said John Hoggott. Stephen and Dick and now in possession of

Mr. Thomas Watson of Yellow Creek Ironworks and are to remain in his possession until the 25th of December next, being hired to Watson for one year. Old Judith is in possession of Mr. Richard Smith of Davidson County and is to remain in his possession until twenty fifth of December next, being hired until that day; Judith, her daughter, is in possession of Mr. Thomas Barnard of Bedford county and is to remain with him until 25 December next, being hired to him for one year which will not expire until that day. 26 April 1814 Abraham Sandifur

Test: Jas. Vaulx, William Quarles

- This Bill of sale proven by the oaths of William Quarles and James Vaulx and ordered Registered. [p139]

HOGGATT, John   Bill of Sale   18 May 1814
I, Abraham Sandifur of Wilson County, do sell to John Hoggatt three negro slaves; Tom about thirty three years of age; Betty, about twenty years of age and Sam, about four years of age. Tom is now in possession of Thomas Watson of Yellow Creek Ironworks and is to remain with him until the 25th of December next, being hired for one year which will not expire until said date; Sam and Betty are to remain in possession of Abraham until January 1st next. 26 April 1814   Abraham Sandifur   Witness: Wm Quarles, Jas. Vaulx
- This Bill of Sale proven by the oath of William Quarles and James Vaulx and ordered Registered. [p140]

HOGGATT, John   Bill of Sale   19 May 1814
I, Abraham Sandifur, have sold to John Hoggatt a negro woman named Amy. 6 March 1811   Abraham Sandifum
Test: Eddm'd Cooper, Williamson Buthright
- This bill of sale was acknowledged by Abraham Sandifur to be his act and deed and ordered Registered. [p141]

ANDERSON, John   Bill of Sale   23 May 1814
I, James G. Martin, have sold John Anderson three negro slaves; one female named Henney, twenty three years, and her child named Abigail aged fifteen months and one boy named Achilles, aged thirteen years.
7 March 1814   J. G. Martin   Test: J. Whiteside, Wm Quarles
- This Bill of Sale was proven by the oath of Jenken Whiteside and William Quarles and ordered Registered. [p142]

TENNESSON, Abraham   Bill of Sale   23 May 1814
I, Abraham Tennassan, Senior, of the county of Rowan and State of North Carolina, have sold to my son, Matthew, a negro boy about sixteen years by the name of Cesar. 15 March 1801

Abraham (X) Tennissan

Test: James (X) Firtpatrick, Samuel Tennisson

- This Bill of Sale was proven by the oath of Samuel Tennisson, one of the subscribing witnesses, the other witness being dead as he believes, and ordered registered. [p1430

PARKER, John C.   Bill of Sale   24 May 1814

I, Robert McGough, have sold to John C. Parker a negro man by the name of Emanuel, between the age of thirty four and thirty five years. 26 April 1814 Robert McGough

- This bill of sale was acknowledged by the said Robert McGough to be his act and deed and ordered registered. [p145]

NICHOLS, John   Bill of Sale   26 May 1814

I. Thomas Henderson of Maryville, Tennessee have sold to John Nichol a negro boy named Neilson, the same I purchased from Stephen Hains of Knoxville, said boy about twenty years old. 22 Dec 1813   Thos. Henderson

Test: David Russell, David Hunter

State of Tennessee - Blount County - December Sessions 1813

- The above bill of sale acknowledged in open court by Thomas Henderson and ordered Registered. [p145]

BARROW, Willie   Bill of Sale   15 June 1814

I, John H. Smith, have sold to Willie Barrow a negro girl named Anny, formerly the property of John W. Clay & was sold by M. C. Dunn, Sheriff on 17 Feb. 1812. 16 Feb. 1814   Jno. H. Smith   Test: Robt Y. Walker

- April Sessions This Bill of Sale acknowledged in open court by the said Smith and ordered Registered. [p146]

BARROW, Willie   Bill of Sale   15 June 1814

I have sold to Willie Barrow a negro man named Peter, which negro man has been for some time in the possession of John E. Beck, Esquire, and which negro I purchased of Miss Sarah E. Harris. 12 Nov. 1813   Thos. K. Harris

Test: J. Whiteside

- April Sessions This Bill of Sale was proven by the oath of Jenkin Whiteside and ordered Registered. [p147]

HARRIS, Thomas K.   Bill of Sale   15 June 1814

I have sold to Thomas K. Harris a certain negro man named Peter, which I inherited from my deceased father . 11 Sept. 1813   Sarah E. Harris

Test: H. G. Harris

- Bill of Sale proven by the oath of Howell G. Harris and ordered registered.

TRIMBLE, James   Bill of Sale   15 June 1814
I, William Shepherd, atty in fact for Samuel Ash and George Davis, Trustees for the heirs of Doratha Marrick in a certain marriage contract entered into by James A. Tabe to said Sam'l Ash and George Davis, as trustees, do hereby convey to Trimble a negro woman named Hariet and her young child, also a mulatto boy named Washington, children of a negro woman called Darcey mentioned in said marriage contract. 29 June 1813   Wm Shepperd
Test: Wm Alexander, W. Barrow
 - July Sessions This bill of sale was proven by the oath of William Alexander and ordered Registered. [p148]

BEARD, Lewis   Power of Attorney   27 June 1814
I, Lewis Beard of the town of Salisbury in Rowan County, State of North Carolina, have appointed Ezra Alleman of the town of Salisbury, Rowan County, NC, my true and lawful attorney - to receive of and from the executors or administrators of Major William T. Lewis, deceased in the State of Tennessee, all such monies due and owning to me. 29 April 1814   LS Beard
  [State of North Carolina - Rowan County] We, being two Justices of the Peace for the County of Rowan do hereby certify that Lewis Beard has personally appeared and acknowledged the above Power of Attorney as his act and deed. 29 April 1814   H. B. Satterwhite, J.P. - J. Murphy, J.P.
  [State of North Carolina - Rowan County] I, John Giles, Clerk of the Court of Pleas and Quarter Sessions, Rowan County do hereby certify that Horace B. Satterwhite and John Murphey are legal acting Justices of the Peace of the county of Rowan. Salisbury 29 April 1814 Jno Giles [ppp150/151]
  [State of North Carolina - Rowan County] This is to certify that John Giles is the Clerk of Rowan County, that he is the keeper of the seal of said Court ...I, John Steel, Chairman of the County Court of Rowan 29 April 1814 [p151]

KINGSLEY, Alpha   Bill of Sale   29 June 1814
I have sold to Alpha Kingsley the following named negroes: Jane and her child Patey; Rebecca and her children, Lucy, Sookey and Anabella. Dorcas, Fanny, Lizza, Ben Mary & Polly to be sold to secure unto the aforesaid Alpha Kingsley which he has loaned me. Capt Kingsley will have the money paid which I owe him out of the before named negroes and the sale of my Island lying in the Tennessee River just above South W. Point and only so much as will pay said debt of three thousand dollars and interest and the residue to be considered mine. 26 Jan'y 1814   Jno Smith   Test: Frans May, Joseph Park
 - May Term This bill of sale proved by the oaths of Francis May and Joseph Park and ordered registered. [p152]

PORTER, George   Bill of Sale   20 July 1814
[State of Kentucky - Logan County] I, Reuben Allen sell to George *Porter, a free man of color, a citizen of the city of Nashville, one mulatto woman by the name of Lydia. 26 December 1810 Reuben Allen
Test: H. Watkins, Senr, Jas. Allen
Nov 29,1812 James Allen acknowledged the last above signature.
- April Session This bill of sale proved by the oath of James Allen and ordered registered. [p153]

NEELEY, S. B.   Bill of Sale   9 August 1814
I, William Neeley, in consideration of the natural love and affection I bear unto Samuel B. Neeley I give unto him the negro slave Jacob, with this reservation, should my dear and affectionate Mother, Jane Neeley, choose to retain the said slave, Jacob, in her possession during her lifetime she is empowered to do so. 26 July 1814   William Neeley Test: Philip Hurt, J. A. Walker
- July Sessions The above Bill of Sale acknowledged in open court by William Neeley and ordered to be registered. [p154]

CATO, Green   Bill of Sale   9 August 1814
I, Mary Cato, widow of Roland Cato, deceased, sell to my son, Green Cato, the following articles: one feather bed and furniture, one bay mare, one loom & spinning wheel, ten head of hogs and all the money due me from sale of property of Roland Cate, deceased, and due me as the widow. 16 February 1814
          Mary (X) Cato   Test: Robert Stringfellow, George Funderburk
- July Sessions   The above Bill of Sale proven by the oaths of Robert Stringfellow and George Funderburk and ordered to be registered. [p155]

McLEMORE, John C.   Bill of Sale   9 August 1814
I, John W. Cocke, have sold to John C. McLemore a negro child named Arianna, three years old. 23 May 1814   J. W. Cocke
Test: Will'm Hart, W. Cannon
- July Sessions This Bill of Sale was proven by the oaths of William C. Hart and W. Cannon and ordered registered. [p156]

KEELING, Leonard   Bill of Sale   9 August 1814
On 8 Sept. 1813 I executed to James Austin a Bill of Sale for twenty four negroes with their increase which was to be void if I or my heirs, should pay the sum of $4288 and all legal costs within five years. Now I transfer and bargain unto Leonard Keeling all the title to said negroes provided said Lenard pay James Austin the said sum of $4288. 16 June 1814   Geo Keeling
Test: Jesse W. Thomas, William Boatright
- July Sessions The above Bill of Sale proven by the oath of Jesse W. Thomas

46

and Williiam Boatright and ordered registered. [p157]

GRAVES, John   Bill of Sale   9 August 1814
Sold to the highest bidder, John Graves, a negro boy, Jacob, to satisfy a judgment
against William Neeley. 19 March 1814   John A. Walker, Constable
- July Sessions The above bill of sale acknowledged by Walker and ordered
registered. [p158]

CARTRIGHT, James   Bill of Sale   9 August 1814
I, Pembroke Cartright, for the natural love and affection I have for my son, James
Cartright, and for one dollar paid in hand by the said James Cartright, sell to
James Cartwright one negro girl, Easter, thirty years old and her increase. 18
July 1814 Pembroke (X) Cartwright Test: Wm C. Robertson, John Cole
- July Sessions The above bill of sale proved by the oaths of William P.
Robertson and John Cole and ordered to be registered. [p159]

CANNON, John J.   Deed of Gift   23 August 1814
I, William Cannon, in consideration of the natural love I bear unto my beloved
son, John J. Cannon, give to him one negro boy named Cyrus, sixteen years old,
bright complection. 2 Nov. 1813 W. Cannon
- Nov. Term This Deed of Gift acknowledged by William Cannon and ordered
registered. [pp159/160]

JONES, Richard   Bill of Sale   28 November 1814
I, John Shelton, have sold to Richard Jones one negro boy four years old, by the
name of Peter. 5 March 1814   John Shelton Aney A. Shelton
Test: G. Wade, Joseph Summers
- July Sessions This Bill of Sale John Shelton and Anney Shelton to Richard
Jones proven by oath of Joseph Sumers, one of the witnesses and ordered
registered. [p161]

PORTER, George   Bill of Sale   28 November 1814
I have sold to George *Porter, a free man of color, a negro boy named Soloman,
about seven years old. 25 August 1814 Leonard Sale
Test: John Woodcock, Geo M. Morten
- October Sessions The above bill of sale proven by the oath of George M.
Morton. [p162]

KINGSLEY, Alpha   Bill of Sale   28 November 1814
A list of property sold this day to Captain Alpha Kingsley: five feather Beds,
Steads & furniture, one side board, one desk & book case, two pair of dining
tables, one pair of tea or breakfast tables, one mahogany tea table, six black

windsor chairs, neatly bottomed or cushioned (needle wrought), forty two plain windsor chairs, one bureau (best quality), one plain bureau, china dining and other table furniture, coffee urn and glassware, kitchen furniture, one waggon and gear complete, one sorrel horse, one bay horse (7 years) one sorrel horse, 5 yrs, one bay mare, one stud horse called Sir Harry, seven cows, 13 young cattle, six sows & pigs, 15 year old shotes, 25 young shotes, 6 weeding hoes, 4 axes, 2 half share plows, 1 large barshare plow, 1 log chair, 1 iron tooth rake, 16 head of sheep. 15 April 1814 Jos Coleman
Test: Jas Brown, Peter Alexander
 -November Term This bill of sale proven by the oaths of James Brown and Peter Alexander and ordered registered. [pp163/164]

KINGSLEY, Alpha   Bill of Sale   28 November 1814
I have sold to Alpha Kingsley a negro man named Ephraim, about thirty five years of age; Stephen, a negro man about twenty six ; a mulatto woman named Pheribee, about twenty years of age; a negro boy named Ferdinand about two years of age. 15 April 1814   Jos Coleman
 - October Sessions This bill of sale Joseph Coleman to Alpha Kingsley was acknowledged by Joseph Coleman. [pp165/166]

JOSLIN, Benj.   Bill of Sale   29 November 1814
We, David Ross and Rolan Allen, late of Warrin County, Mississippi Territory, sold Benj. Joslin the following negros; one negro man called Magis, one negro woman called Pheobe, 36 head of cattle, one hundred and thirty head of hoggs, together with an improvement where said Ross now lives and all household and kitchen furniture. 21 June 1814 David Ross, R. Allen
Test: C. Stump, Tho. Hickman
 - October Sessions This bill of sale proved by the oath of Christopher Stump and Thomas Hickman and ordered registered. [p167]

SMILEY, Robert   Bill of Sale   12 December 1814
I, Jasper Sutton of the county of Maury and State of Tennessee, have sold to Robert Smiley a negro man named Charles, about forty five years old and his wife, a negro woman named Suckey, about thirty years of age and their child, a negro boy named Stephen, about three months of age. 28 October 1814
       Jasper Sutton   Wit: Henry C. Ewin
 - October Sessions This Bill of Sale was acknowledged by Jasper Sutton and ordered to be registered. [p168]

PATTERSON, Gideon   Bill of Sale   13 December 1814
I, Gideon Patison, have given to my children, John, Hillery, Nancy, Langford,

David, James, Sally and Mead, four negroes; Lucy, Berry, King & Phillip to be equally divided between my seven children, together with any increase of said negroes, the whole of my stock and household furniture.
19 August 1814   Gideon Patterson   Test: R. G. Foster, John Robison
- October Sessions   This Bill of Sale acknowledged by Gideon Pattison and ordered registered. [p169]

JACKSON, James   In Trust   13 December 1814
I, Thomas Kirkman, sell to James Jackson a negro girl named Peggy, about eighteen years of age of a light black colour; to the use of Elizabeth McKarrahan.
30 September 1814   Thos Kirkman   Test: James Erwin, Richard Cockran
- September Sessions Bill of Sale Thomas Kirkman to James Jackson in trust for Elizabeth McKarrahon, proved by the oath of James Erwin and Richard Cockran and ordered registered. [pp170/171]

KENNEDY, Isaac   Bill of Sale   13 December 1814
I have sold to Isaac Kennedy one negro woman named Jinny, about eighteen years old. 13 Sept. 1814   Jno. H. Gibson
Wit: Duncan Robertson, W. Tait
- October Sessions This bill of sale proven by the oath of Duncan Robertson and William Tait and ordered registered. [p171]

NICHOL, John   Bill of Sale   15 December 1814
Lexington, Kentucky August 1, 1814. I, John J. Cannon (late of Nashville) sold John Nichol of Nashville a certain negro boy by the name of Cyrus, of a light complexion, about fifteen or sixteen years old.   John J. Cannon
Witness: Geo Poyzer
  I, William Cannon, do hereby certify the within bill of sale and hereby for myself and John J. Cannon covenant that the same shall be good in law.
12 August 1814   W. Cannon
Witness: James C. Craig, Nicholas Hobson
- October Sessions The above bill of sale proven by the oath of George Poyzer and ordered registered. [pp172/173]

ROPER, Richard   Bill of Sale   15 December 1814
I, George W. Clingham, have sold to Richard Roper a negro girl named Lidy, aged four, yellow complection. 14 October 1814   Geo. W. Clingham
Test: Wm Linsster
- October Sessions This bill of sale probed by the oath of William Lainster and ordered registered. [pp173/174]

WHITESIDE, Jinkin   Bill of Sale   16 January 1815
I, Joseph Coleman, have sold to Jinkin Whiteside one light coloured negro man
named Bob, by trade a blacksmith, thirty two years old. 18 October 1813
Jos Coleman   Test: Washington Perkins, William Quarles
- October Sessions This bill of sale was proven by the oath of Washington
Perkins and William Quarles and ordered registered. [pp174/175]

TURNER, Lemuel T.   Bill of Sale   16 February 1815
I, John S. Williamson have sold to Lemuel T. Turner one negro girl named Aney,
about twelve or thirteen years old. 1 January 1815   John S. Williamson Test
J. Roans, Thos. Williamson
- January Sessions The above bill of sale proven by the oath of James Roane
and Thomas Williamson and ordered registered. [p176]

TURNER, Lemuel T.   Bill of Sale   16 February 1815
I, C. Stump, have sold to L. T. Turner a negro woman called Sarah, aged forty
five or fifty. 3 Dec. 1815   C. Stump   Teste: Joseph McKean
- January Sessions The above bill of sale acknowledged by Christopher Stump
and ordered to be registered. [p177]

HEWETT, C.   Bill of Sale   16 February 1815
I, Polly Maddox, have sold unto Caleb Hewitt a negro woman named Ana and
a child named Peggy; said woman 23 years of age and the child about eighteen
months. 4 Jan. 1815 Polly Maddox   Test: Ellis Maddox, Robert Stainbock
- January Sessions This bill of sale proven by the oath of Ellis Maddox and
Robert Stainbock and ordered registered. [p178]

BOYD, George W.   Bill of Sale   18 February 1815
I, John Lanier, constable for the county of Davidson, by virtue of the following
executions (three at the instant of George W. Boyd; one at the instance of David
Moore and Joseph T. Elliston ane at the instance of William Pitt Bowers, one at
the instance of Archabold Scott) all against Jeramiah Hinton have sold the
following property: Winch named Poll and her sucking child, also sold to George
W. Boyd one other negro girl, a child of Poll by the name of Charity, also to
Boyd one bed, bedstead & furniture, one other bed & furniture, one bureau, one
cupboard & furniture, one small chest, one dozen chairs, one set of dining tables,
also four dutch ovens, two pots, two pot racks, two kittles, four pair of pot hooks,
one pair of waffle irons, one grid iron, two pair of shovels and tons, two pair of
fire irons, one skillet, four pails, two tubbs & churn, four candlesticks, 30 head
of hogs, stud horse *Rusty Robbin*. 16 Jan 1815   John Lanier, Constable
- January Sessions This bill of sale acknowledged by Lanier as constable and
ordered registered. [pp179/180]

BOYD, John   Bill of Sale   18 February 1815
I, John Lanier, Constable, have sold the following property to John Boyd, he being the highest bidder:
Alford, a negro boy supposed about seven; also another negro boy about four years old by the name of Olliver; seven head of cattle. 16 January 1815 John Lanier, Constable   Teste: D. Young, H. Douglass
- January Sessions   This bill of sale acknowledged by Lanier and ordered registered. [pp181/182]

PORTER, George   Bill of Sale   18 February 1815
We, George W. Clingan and Charlotte Clingan sell unto Porter a negro woman called Amey. 12 December 1814   George W. Clingan   Charlotte Clingan Teste: Jno Moore, R. Allen
- January Sessions   This bill of sale probed by the oath of John Moore and ordered registered. [p182]

GRAVES, Henry   Bill of Sale   18 February 1815
We, Isham Davis and Jesse Holt of Wilson County have sold to Henry Graves a negro woman slave about twenty seven, of a black complexion, also her children, a boy about three years old by name of Jerry. 4 August 1814
Isham Davis   Jesse Holt   Witness: John Dew, Arthur L. Davis
- January Sessions   This bill of sale proven by the oaths of John Dew and Arthur L. Davis and ordered registered. [p183]

ANDERSON, William P.   Bill of Sale   26 April 1815
I, Wm Anderson, of the County of Davidson & State of Tennessee, late of the Commonwealth of Kentucky, have sold to Wm P. Anderson of the town of Nashville a negro man named Harry, which said negro fellow has for some time been in the possession of Patton Anderson of the County of Botetourt and Commonwealth of Virginia on loan. 6 May 1803   Wm Anderson
Test: J. Preston , A. Taylor
[Virginia] At a Superior Court held for Henrico County at the Capital in the City of Richmond 15 Sept 1812, this Bill of Sale was proved by the oath of John Preston & ordered to be certified to the state of Tennessee. John Robinson, Clerk
I, William Brackinbraugh, Judge of the Superior Court for the County of Henrico do certify the attestation of John Robinson who is the Clerk of the aforesaid Court. 15 March 1814   W. Brackinbraugh
[Virginia] At a Court held for the County of Botetourt the 9th of November 1814 the annexed Bill of Sale was proven by the oath of Allin Taylor another witness thereto and ordered certified in the state of Tennessee. Henry Bawyer, Clerk

[Botetourt County] I, Matthew Harvey presiding magistrate of said court do certify that the foregoing attestation of Henry Bawyer, Clerk of said court is in due form. 10 Nov. 1814 Matthew Harvey [pp184/185]

WEAKLEY, Samuel   Bill of Sale   29 April 1815
I, Michael C. Dunn, Sheriff for the county of Davidson, by virtue of a writ to me directed from the County Court of Rutherford County, (Daniel L. Henderson and Bennet Henderson against William T. Henderson),
I have levied the same on a negro boy child about three years of the name of Alexander, and after advertising did offer for sale on 7 January 1815., at which sale Samuel Weakley was the highest bidder & became the purchaser.
14 February 1815 M. C. Dunn, Sheriff of Davidson Cty
-April Sessions The above Bill of Sale acknowledged by M. C. Dunn and ordered registered. [pp186/187]

ELAM, Samuel   Bill of Sale   2 May 1815
I, Alexander Ewing, have this day sold to Samuel Elam a negro woman slave about thirty four or five years of age, by the name of Nancy. 7 Feb. 1815
Alexander Ewing   Test: Tho. H. Fletcher, Q. McKiernan
- April Sessions. The above Bill of Sale acknowledged by said Ewing and ordered registered. [p187]

ELAM, Samuel   Bill of Sale   2 May 1815
I Nicholas B. Pryor, have sold Samuel Elam a negro boy slave about six years old by the name of Tom. 1 November 1814 N. B. Pryor
Teste: Harbert Walker
- April Session This Bill of Sale acknowledged by said Pryor and ordered registered. [p188]

SPEICE, Lewis   Bill of Sale   2 May 1815
I, John Shelton have sold to Lewis Speice a certain negro girl by the name of Caty. 24 April 1814 John Shelton Amey Shelton
Teste: Tho. Hardy, Levy (X) Claybrook
- April Sessions This Bill of Sale, John Shelton and Amey Shelton was proven by the oaths of Thomas Hardy and Levy Claybrook and ordered registered. [p189]

GREER, Benjamin   Bill of Sale   2 May 1815
I, John W. Moran, have sold to Benjamin Greer a negro fellow by the name of Luke, thirty five years of age. 18 February 1815 John W. Moran Witness: J. W. Horton, James (X) Donnelly
- April Sessions The above bill of sale proven by the oath of Joseph W. Horton. [p190]

BREWER, Sterlong   Bill of Sale   2 May 1815
I, William Peacock, have this day sold to Stirlong Brewer of Dickson County and the State of Tennessee a negro woman by the name of Delilah and her male child named Gibbins. 25 April 1815 Wm Peacock
Witness: Michl Matton, Sarah Pearsall
   -April Sessions This bill of sale was acknowledged by the said William Peacock and ordered registered. [p192]

THOMAS, Philip   Bill of Sale   8 May 1815
We, Josiah Jackson and William Jackson of Wilson County and State of Tennessee, have sold to Philip *Thomas [free man mulatto] of Davidson County one negro girl (black colour) about the age of twenty by the name of Fanny who formerly belonged to Obadiah Jackson of said last mentioned county.
30 July 1814   Josiah Jackson   William Jackson
Test: Henry Crabb, Henry Cromer, Nathaniel Peck
 - April Sessions This bill of sale was proven by the oath of Henry Cromer and Nathaniel Peck and ordered registered. [p193]

LEE, Braxton   Bill of Sale   15 May 1815
I, Lewis Henry Lee, have sold unto Braxton Lee all of my claim to my father, Stephen Lee, deceased, estate which he left to me in his last will and testament. 16 February 1813   Lewis Henry Lee
Test: Abraham (X) Tippsey, Manuel Hunting
 - April Sessions The above bill of sale proven by the oath of Abraham and Manuel Hunting and ordered registered. [p194]

LEE, Braxton   Bill of Sale   15 May 1815
I, Thomas Hickman, have sold to Braxton Lee a negro woman by the name of Patience, about twenty. 7 Jan. 1812   Tho. Hickman
 Wit: Russell Gower, Jas. Curtis
 - April Sessions This bill of sale was acknowledged by Thomas Hickman and ordered registered. [p195]

LEE, Braxton   Bill of Sale   15 May 1815
I, James Lovell, have sold to Braxton Lee a negro boy, eleven years old, named Jacob. 2 Dec. 1814   Jas Lovell   Attest: Abraham Tippey, Elijah Spiller
 - April Sessions This bill of sale acknowledged in open court by the said James Lovell and ordered registered. [p196]

WEAKLEY, R.   Bill of Sale   10 July 1815
I, Henry Garnett of King and Queen County and State of Virginia, have sold to Robert Weakley of Davidson County and State of Tennessee, the following negroes: Tom, about thirty two years old last January; Aggy, his wife, about

twenty seven years old; Betty, about nine years old; Duie, about seven years old; Judy, about six years old; General, a boy about four; Amy, about three years old; Violet, about two years old; Sally about seven months. 16 August 1814   Henry Garnett   Teste: E. Talbot, Wm Cole, Thomas Talbot
- January Sessions   This deed was proven by the oath of Thomas Talbot
- April Sessions   This deed of sale Henry Garnett to Robert Weakley proven by the oath of Eli Talbot & ordered to be registered. [pp197/198]

FRASHER, George   Bill of Sale   21 July 1815
We, Jane Trotter and Moses A. Locke of Rowan County and State of North Carolina, administrators of Richard Trotter, deceased sell to George Fisher of the same county and state the two following described negroes; Tom, a black fellow about forty years of age and Jack, a mulatto fellow about twenty seven years of age. Jack is a house carpenter and Tom is a handy fellow as a farmer or as a house servant. 16 Oct. 1812   Jane Trotter Moses A. Locke
Teste: Joseph Chambers
[State of NC Rowan County] Nov. Term 1814   I, John Giles, Clerk of the County Court of Pleas & Quarter Sessions of Rowan certify the within bill was duly proven by the oath of Joseph Chambers, recorded & ordered to be registered. Jno. Giles
[State of NC - Rowan County] I hereby certify the above bill of sale is duly registered in the Registers office in Book No 32, page 159. 4 Feb 1815 Hugh Braley
[State of NC - Rowan County] I, Lewis Beard, Presiding Magistrate do hereby certify that John Giles, Esqr is the Clerk of Rowan County and he is the keeper of the seal of Court 7 Feb. 1815 D. Beard P Clk [pp198/200]

GREIR, Benjamin   Covenant   22 August 1815
I, James Donly of Davidson County, am firmly bound unto Benjamin Grier and Margaret his wife. The conditions of the above obligation is such if the above James Donly shall by his last will and testament provide that one half of his estate shall be vested in the said Greir and his wife and her/his heirs precisely in the same way and manner as tho the said Margaret and her brother John were the only heirs of said James, except that the widows dower should the said James wife survive him or rather the one half thereof shall not vest until her death. It is further understood that no conveyance or transfer is to be made by the said James in his lifetime to evade this obligation, then this obligation to be void. James (X) Donley   14 Feb. 1815   Teste: Felix Grundy, John Shute
- April Sessions This Covenant proven by the oath of Felix Grundy and ordered registered. [pp200/201]

NICHOL, John   Bill of Sale   1 Sept. 1815
I, Beal Bosley, for and in consideration of the natural love and affection I bear

my daughter Rachael and her husband John Nichol and also in consideration of $250.00 to be paid before the delivery, have sold the following described negro slaves: Austin, about thirty years old & Fanny, about twenty two years old; Ned, her son, about five years old, Matilda, her daughter, about three and a half years old, Osmund, her son about ten months old; also a girl named Polly about sixteen years old. 7 Feb 1813 Beal Bosley   Test: Nicholas Hobson
- July Sessions The above bill of sale proven by the oath of Nicholas Hobson and ordered registered. [p202]

GLEAVES, Michael   Bill of Sale   1 Sept 1815
I have sold unto Michael Gleaves a certain negro man slave aged nineteen years. July 18, 1815   William McCabe   Wit: James H. Gamble
- July Sessions   This bill of sale was acknowledged by William McCabe and ordered registered. [p203]

WILLIAMSON, John S.   Bill of Sale   1 Sept. 1815
I, Jasper Sutton of the State of Tennessee and County of Maury, have sold unto John S. Williamson of the state of Tennessee and county of Davidson one negro boy by the name of Phillip, aged five years. 22 July 1815   Jasper R. Sutton Teste: Walter Kieble
- July Sessions this bill of sale acknowledged by Jasper Sutton and ordered registered. [p204]

McGREGOR, Flower   Bill of Sale   1 Sept 1815
I, Thomas Overton, have sold to Flower McGregor five negroes; Cherry, Bill, Zeland, Sally and Daniel. 2 Jan 1813   Tho. Overton
- July Sessions 1815   This bill of sale acknowledged by the said Thomas Overton and ordered to be registered. [p205]

RUTLAND, Blake   Bill of Sale   1 Sept. 1815
I, George Martin, have sold to Blake Rutland and Isham F. Davis of the County of Wilson and State of Tennessee a certain negro woman named Amy, a negro boy named Joe, and also a negro girl named Genia and also all the right and claim I have to the land that James McCay now lives on and also three beds and furniture, also one judgment on Lewis Allin, also one judgment on Francis L. Ross . 4 Sept. 1812   George Martin   Test: Elijah Maddox, Wiley Alford
- The condition of the above obligation is such that if George Martin does pay the said Rutland and Davis before the 4th day of Sept. 1813, with interest, the above obligation to be void. 4 Sept 1812
Elijah Maddox, Wiley Alford   Blake Rutland, Isham F. Davis
- July Sessions This deed of sale was proven by the oath of Elijah Maddox and William Alford and ordered registered. [pp206/207

PORTER, Alex'r   Bill of Sale   19 Sept 1815
I, Michael C. Dunn, Sheriff of Davidson County, by virtue of a writ directed
from the County Court of Rutherford County (Daniel L. Henderson & Bennett
Henderson agst William T. Henderson) have levied same on two negroes as the
property of William T. Henderson; one boy named John, aged about fifteen and
one boy named Sam, about thirteen and after advertising ...on 7 January 1815
Alexander Porter became purchaser of same. 10 Jan. 1815 M. C. Dunn, Sheff
Test: C. Stump, E. Raworth
 - January Sessions This bill of sale was acknowledged by Michael C. Dunn and
ordered registered. [p209]

BROWN, Bedford   Power of Attorney   12 Oct. 1815
I, Bedford Brown of the State of Georgia and County of Clark, have appointed
my trusty friend William Trigg, of the County of Sumner and State of Tennessee,
my true and lawful attorney and in my name relinquish my claim to two hundred
and fifty acres of land to John Davis. The said land was conveyed to me by John
Davis on 18 July 1798 and is lying in the county of -------- on Big Harpeth River
near the mouth of South Harpeth and adjoining Patrick Quiglyes preemption.
3 Oct. 1814 Bedford Brown   Test: James Davis
 - August Term The foregoing Power of Attorney was duly proven by the oath
of James Davis and ordered registered. [pp209/210]

BOSLEY, Beal   Bill of Sale   19 Oct. 1815
I, John Nichol, have sold to Beal Bosley a negro girl named Polly, being the
same the said Beal Bosley conveyed to me per Bill of Sale dated 17 Feb. 1815.
18 Oct. 1815 Jno. Nichol Test: Nich's Hobson, Nathan Ewing, H. C. Ewin
 - October Sessions This bill of sale proven by oath of Nathan Ewing and Henry
C. Ewin and ordered registered. [p211]

GREER, Martin   Bill of Sale   4 Dec. 1815
I, Hosa League, have sold Martin Greer a negro woman and her future increase
by the name of Charlotte, twenty one years old. 7 May 1815   Hosa League
  Teste: Robert Thomas, Joseph Greer
 - October Sessions This bill of sale proven by the oath of Robert Thomas and
Joseph Greer and ordered registered. [p212]

CARTWRIGHT, James   Bill of Sale   4 Dec. 1815
I, Pembrook Cartwright, in consideration of esteem and affection I have for my
son, James Cartwright, and the further consideration of one dollar, have sold to
the said James three negroes; Josie about twenty eight years of age, William
about three years of age and Fanny, an infant. 14 Sept 1815
     Pembrook (X) Cartwright
Teste: Samuel L. Wharton, William Call, John Call

- October Sessions This bill of sale was proven by the oath of William Cale and John Cale and ordered registered. [p213]

CHILDRESS, Thomas   Bill of Sale   8 Feb. 1816
I, Fleming Gatewood, of the State of Kentucky, have sold to Thomas Childress of the Town of Nashville a negro man slave by the name of Dick, about eighteen years old. 17 Feb. 1815   Fleming Gatewood   Teste: S. Cowan, Jr.
- January Sessions - This bill of sale proved by the oath of S. Cowan, Junr and ordered registered. [p214]

TRIMBLE, James   Bill of Sale   8 Feb. 1816
I, John B. Guathney, sell to James Trimble and Alfred Balch a certain negro man named Jacob, at present in the possession of Andrew Morrison as a boatman. 19 Jan. 1816   J. B. Guathney   Test: E. Benoit
- January Sessions This bill of sale proven by the oath of Ernest Benoit and ordered registered. [p215]

HENRY, William   Bill of Sale   8 Feb. 1815
I, Henry Brown, have sold to William Henry one negro woman slave named Dolly about twenty seven years of age and one child 2 weeks old of said woman. 24 Jan. 1814   Henry Brown   Teste: Hugh Allison, Alexander Henry
- January Sessions This Bill of Sale proven by the oath of Hugh Allison and Alexander Henry and ordered registered. [p216]

DRAKE, Joseph   Bill of Sale   8 Feb. 1816
I, Green Cato, have sold to Joseph Drake a negro girl named Caty, about four years old. 1 Nov. 1815   Green Cato   Test: Jesse Smith, Enis Marriss
- January Sessions This bill of sale proven by the oath of Jesse Smith, one of the witnesses, and ordered registered. [p217]

McLEMORE, John C.   Bill of Sale   8 Feb. 1816
I, Felix Allen, have sold to John C. McLemore a negro woman named Lucy, of the age of twenty one years and her child Nanny, about 10 months old. 20 Nov. 1815   Felix Allen   Test: Nathan Ewing, Henry C. Ewing
- Jan'y Sessions This bill of sale proved by the oath of Nathan Ewing and Henry C. Ewing and ordered registered. [p218]

HENRY, William   Bill of Sale   8 Feb. 1816
I, Newsom Barham, have sold to William Henry a negro girl named Silvy, about nineteen years old. 30 Sept 1815   Newsom Barham   Test: Hugh Allison
- January Sessions This bill of sale acknowledged by the said Newsom Barham and ordered registered. [p219]

NICHOLS, John   Bill of Sale   9 Feb. 1816
I, John Street, of the County of Bedford and State of Tennessee, have sold to
John Nichols a negro man named Ben, about fifty years of age. 15 Jan. 1816
          Jno T. Street   Test: E. Benoit, T. Weston
 - January Sessions This bill of sale proved by the oath of Ernest Benoit and
Thomas Weston and ordered registered. [p220]

BARROW, Matthew   Bill of Sale   9 Feb. 1816
I, John Braham, have sold to Matthew Barrow a negro woman named Milly,
about eighteen years of age and her infant daughter Betsey, five months old.
 3 June 1811   John Braham   Test: Boyd McNairy, Horace Greene
 - January Session This bill of sale proven by the oath of Boyd McNairy and
Horace Green and ordered registered. [p221]

BARROW, Matthew   Bill of Sale   9 Feb. 1816
I, Edwin H. Childress, have sold to Matthew Barrow a negro man about twenty
one years of age, named Nelson. 4 Jan 1816   Edwin H. Childress
Test: Jno. C. McLemore, J. Blackfan
 - January Sessions This bill of sale was proven by the oath of John C.
McLemore and Jesse Blackfan and ordered registered. [p222]

McDANIEL, Clement   Bill of Sale   21 Feb. 1816
I, Clement McDaniel, sell to Alexander Richardson a negro man named Aaron,
about twenty seven years of age. 23 Feb. 1814 Clement McDaniel
Teste: Wm Alexander
RICHARDSON, Alexander [transfer of the above slave] July 12, 1814 This
day I have sold to Robert Weakley all my interest in the above contract.
          Alex. Richardson
 - January Sessions This bill of sale for negro man, Aaron, proven by the oath
of William Alexander and a receipt [Alexander Richardson to Robert Weakley]
acknowledged by Weakley and ordered registered. [pp223/224]

WEAKLEY, Robert   Bill of Sale   21 Feb. 1816
We, Gabriel Loving and Sarah Loving, his wife, have sold to Robert Weakley a
negro woman by the name of Nelly, about eighteen. August 22, 1814 Gabriel
Loving   Sarah (X) Loving   Teste: Edward Richardson
 - January Sessions   This bill of sale acknowledged by Gabriel Loving and
ordered to be certified. [p224]

HOOD, James   Bill of Sale   14 March 1816
I, James Terrell of the County of Giles and State of Tennessee, have sold to
James Hood of Davidson County, a negro boy slave about eighteen years old,
named Nelson. 22 November 1815   James Terrell

Teste: R. T. Walker, Ethelbert Sanders

- January Sessions This bill of sale proved by the oath of Robert T. Walker and Ethelbert Sanders and ordered to be registered. [p225]

HARVEY, Charles - agent of James Harvey Covenant   27 April 1816
I, Edward Hogon of the County of Jackson and State of Tennessee and bound unto Charles Harvey, agent of James Harvey of the Town of Lewisburg, North Carolina.   The condition of the above obligation is ... Charles Harvey is to deliver unto me a bill of sale from James Harvey of the town of Lewisburg, N.C. for a negro man named Gilbert, about thirty years of age as also a negro woman, named Polly, and her four children. 27 June 1815 Edward Hogin Test: William Neely

- April Sessions This Covenant proven by the oath of William Neeley and ordered recorded. [pp226/227]

WEAKLEY, Robert   Memorandum of Agreement   15 May 1816
Peter LeGrand does convey to Robert Weakley the following negro slaves: Jack, aged about thirty eight; Molly, about thirty five years, and her five children - Nancy, Harriet, Jack, Billy & an infant called Matilda. If LeGrand shall pay his debt this agreement to be void. 12 Nov. 1812 Peter LeGrand R. Weakley
Teste: Jno. Dickinson

- Jan 6, 1812 Rec'd payment in full Peter LeGrand

Test: James Jackson, Alexr McCullock, S. Crostwaight

- January Sessions The above agreement was proven by the oath of James Jackson and Alexander McCullock and ordered registered.

- April Sessions The above agreement being produced in open court and it appearing to the court that John Dickinson the subscribing witness is dead, the handwriting of said witness was proven by Ephraim H. Foster & swears he was well acquainted with the handwriting of said Dickinson ... ordered registered.[pp227/229

CROSWEY, John   Bill of Sale   18 May 1816
I, John Bysor, sell to John Nicholas Croswey a negro girl named Lucy, between ten and twelve years of age. 8 May 1813   John Bysor
Teste: John Thomas, Thomas Talbot, Sam Elam

- January Sessions This bill of sale proved by the oath of Thomas Talbot and Samuel Elam & ordered registered. [p230]

STUMP, C.   Bill of Sale   18 May 1816
We, Benjamin Hendricks, Archabald M. Campbell, both of the State of Kentucky and County of Logan have sold to C. Stump a family of negroes named as follows: negro man, Harry, about forty; his wife, Charlott, aged twenty five; also her two children, Jack, aged six or seven; Smith, about three years old.

25 April 1816.   Benj. Hendricks   A. M. Campbell   Teste:
- April Sessions This bill of sale acknowledged by Benjamin and Archibald M. to be their act and ordered registered. [p231]

KINGSLEY, Alpha Memorandum of Household Furniture sold   18 May 1816
Sold by William Chandler to Alpha Kingsley this 14th day of February 1816:
1 sett knives & forks; 2 sad irons, 1 coffee pot, 7 gr sugar, 1 sett of cups & saucers, 2 pr of scissors, 1 chissel and 2 tin cups, 3 bowls & 1 pitcher, 1 sugar bowl and cream pot, 1 hand saw, 1 drawing knife, 1 trowel, 1 iron square, 1 pr #10 and 1 pr #5 cards, 1 bed and begging, 1 bureau, 1 ladies saddle, 1 sett silver teaspoons, 93 cedar logs. Received of Alpha Kingsley fifty dollars in a horse and the balance of $95.32 in money this 14 Feb. 1816   William Chandler
Wit: Tho. B. Tunstall, P. Alexander
- April Sessions This bill of sale acknowledged by said William and ordered registered. [pp232/233]

GARNER, John   Indenture   27 May 1816
I, Edward A. Keeling of the County of Williamson, sell to John Garner the following slaves: Daril, about 16; Daphne, about twenty four; Thomas about six; Horace, about three; Haley, about one year old..children of said Daphne. Edward A. Keeling has been served with a writ issued from the Court of Pleas & Quarter Sessions of Davidson County - said writ being issued at instance of William Wharton against said Keeling for debt of thirteen hundred and seventy dollars ... Garner is bond for Keeling . If Keeling is exonerated this obligation to be void. 25 Dec. 1815 E. A. Keeling Test: James McCrea, Jno Iredale
- January Sessions This deed of mortgage proved by the oath of James McCrea and John Iredale and ordered registered. [pp234/235]

EDMONDSON, Rob.   Power of Attorney   28 May 1816
I, George Titus, appoint my friend Robert Edmondson my true and lawful attorney ... to sell or dispose of any personal property that I have within the limits of West Tennessee or elsewhere. 21 Dec. 1810   George Titus
Test: A. J. Edmondson, B. Searcy, Peter Wright
- April Sessions - This Power of Attorney proven by the oath of A. J. Edmondson and Peter Wright and ordered registered. [pp236/237

EDMONDSON, Isabella   Deed of Relinquishment   28 May 1816
We, William Edmondson, Andrew J. Edmondson, James Titus, Peter Wright, George Titus and Rebecca Edmondson, distributees of the estate of Isabella Edmondson, late of Davidson County, deceased, do give to Isabella Edmondson, one of the legatees of said dec'd all title to one negro woman slave named Betty. 28 March 1816   Wm Edmondson, James Titus, Peter Wright, George Titus, George Titus, Rebeckah Edmondson, A. J. Edmondson

Teste: William Edmondson, John Fitzhugh
- April Sessions This deed of relinquishment proven by the oath of William
Edmondson and John Fitzhugh and ordered registered. [p238]

EDMONDSON, Andrew   Bill of Sale   7 June 1816
I, Robert Edmondson, have sold to Andrew Jackson Edmondson two negro boys
and one negro girl; one negro boy named Arnol, about nineteen; the other boy
named Elam, about thirteen; the girl named Rody about fourteen years of age.
13 Feb. 1816 Robt Edmondson Test: Wm Black, James McCutchan
- April Sessions This bill of sale proved by the oath of William Black and
James McCutchan and ordered registered. [p239]

LOVELL, James   Bill of Sale   7 June 1816
I, John C. House have sold to James Lovell two negro boys; one a girl named
Lucy, fourteen years old; the other a boy named Jacob, eleven years old.
16 Nov. 1814 John C. House   Teste: Nicholas Young, Philip Grimes
-April Sessions This bill of sale acknowledged by the said John C. to be his act
and ordered to be registered.[p240]

SUMNERS, Duke W.   Bill of Sale   7 June 1816
I, John Bryan, have sold to Duke W. Sumner a certain negro woman slave by the
name of Selah. 9 Jan. 1816 John Bryan   Test: William Brooks
- April Sessions This Bill of Sale was proven by the oath of William Brooks
and ordered registered. [p241]

BLACK, William   Bill of Sale   10 June 1816
I, William L. Boyd, sell to William Black a negro man named Benjamin, about
twenty two or three years of age. 13 April 1816   W. L. Boyd
Teste: Geo. Poyzer
- April Sessions This bill of sale was acknowledged by the said William L. and
ordered registered. [p242]

McCLURE, William   Bill of Sale   10 June 1816
I, James Stewart, have sold to William McClure a fellow named Sandy aged 27.
22 Dec. 1815   James Stewart   Teste: J. M. Singleton
- April Sessions This bill of sale acknowledged by the said James and ordered
registered. [p243]

LEWIS, William B.   Bill of Sale   10 June 1816
I, Thomas Crutcher, sell to William B. Lewis two negro boys named Jacob and
Washington. 30 March 1816 Tho. Crutcher   Teste: Jno. H. Eaton
- April Sessions This bill of sale proven by the oath of John H. Eaton and
ordered registered. [p244]

EDMONDSON, Rebecca   Bill of Sale   10 June 1816
I, Robert Edmondson have sold to Rebecca Edmondson a negro girl by the name
of Patt, eighteen years of age. 13 Feb. 1816   Robt Edmondson
Teste: Wm Black, James McCutchen
 - April Sessions This bill of sale was proven by the oath of William Black and
James McCutchen and ordered registered. [p245]

EDMONDSON, Isabella   Bill of Sale   10 June 1816
I have sold to Isabella Edmondson a negro girl named Mary, aged five years old.
29 Dec. 1812   Robt Edmondson   Teste: Peter Wright
 - April Sessions This bill of sale was proven by the oath of Peter Wright and
ordered registered. [p246]

SUMNER, Exum   Bill of Sale   10 June 1816
I, John S. Butler, have sold to Exum Sumner one negro man named Peter, aged
twenty eight years. 26 Nov. 1815   J. S. Butler   Teste: Wm Gilchrist
 - April Sessions This bill of sale was proven by the oath of William Gilchrist
and ordered registered. [p247]

BOSWORTH, William   Bill of Sale   11 June 1816
We, Joel Jones of the County of Williamson and State of Tennessee, and James
Pitman of the County of Buckingham and State of Virginia, have sold William
Bosworth a negro boy slave by the name of Philip, now in my possession, about
nine years of age. 17 April 18..   Joel W. Jones James Pittman
Teste: Thomas Brock
 - April Sessions This bill of sale was acknowledged by the said Jones and
Pitman and ordered registered. [pp248/249]

WHITE, Joshua   Bill of Sale   11 June 1816
I have sold Joshua White a negro woman named Lency, and her child called
Sookey. 5 Jan. 1816 Howell G. Harris Wit: Wilson White, George N. Lyle
 - Jan'y Sessions This bill of sale proven by the oath of Wilson White and
George N. Lyle and ordered registered. [p249]

CRABB, Henry   Bill of Sale   11 June 1816
I, Henry Crabb, to Philip Thomas a negro boy slave named Dave, about nine or
ten years of a black colour and strong made. 9 March 1816 Henry Crabb
Teste: Jacob Shall, John L. Hadley
 -April Sessions This bill of sale was acknowledged by Henry Crabb and
ordered registered. [p250]

THOMAS, Philip   Bill of Sale   11 June 1816
I have sold to Philip Thomas a negro boy slave named Edmond aged twelve

years. 31 May 1815 Th. Yeatman Wit: Nath. S. Anderson, Geo. Poyzer
- April Sessions This bill of sale was acknowledged by Thomas Yeatman to be
his act and ordered registered. [p251]

BREWER, Sterling   Bill of Sale   11 June 1816
I, Thomas Williamson, have sold to Sterling Brewer of Dickson County, TN, a
negro girl slave named Anney, about eleven years old.
8 August 1814   Thomas Williamson   Witness: Tho. Childress
- April Sessions This bill of sale was proven by the oath of
Thomas Childress and ordered to be so certified. [p252]

RUTHERFORD, Felix   Bill of Sale   5 August 1816
We, John Bowden and John Robertson, have sold to Felix Rutherford, of the
County of Williamson, a negro woman about eighteen years of age and her
daughter Jenny about one year of age. 7 June 1816
            John Bowden   John Robeson
Wit: Chas McKerabon, Sam'l McChesney
- July Sessions This bill of sale was proven by the oath of Charles McKerabon
and Samuel McChesney and ordered to be registered. [p253]

BOYD, George W.   Bill of Sale   5 August 1816
I, Coll McNeil, have sold to George W. Boyd a negro boy slave by the name of
Cato, about ten or eleven years old. 30 January 1816   Coll McNeil
Wit: J. L. Young, Robert M. Hood
- July Sessions This bill of sale was proven by the oath of John L. Young and
ordered registered. [p254]

CAMPBELL, James   Bill of Sale   5 August 1816
I, Thomas Garrett, have sold to James Campbell a negro woman named Phillis,
about twenty nine years of age and her child Richard. 2 Jan. 1816
Thos. Garrett   Wit: James Trimble, James P. Clark
- April Sessions This bill of sale was proven by the oath of James Trimble and
James P. Clark and ordered to be registered. [p255]

WHITE, John   Bill of Sale   5 August 1816
I, Elizabeth Smith, have sold to Doctor John White of the County of Williamson,
a certain negro girl named Lucinda, about fourteen months old. 6 July 1816
Elizabeth (E) Smith [her mark]   Wit: P. Lyon, A. Wilson
- This bill of sale was acknowledged by the said Elizabeth Smith as her act and
ordered to be registered. [p256]

HARRIS, Elizabeth   Bill of Sale   30 Aug. 1816
I have this day sold to Elizabeth Harris a negro woman named Cate and a small

63

girl Hetta, which negroes were apportioned to Anna Harris, dec'd, a minor, from the estate of Howell Harris, deceased. 3 Jan. 1816 Howell G. Harris Witt L W. Barrow

- April Sessions This bill of sale was proven by the oath of Willie Barrow and ordered registered. [p257]

LYON, John   Agreement   Sept 18, 1816
Article of Agreement made 7 February 1815 between L. L. Henderson and John Lyon: L. L. Henderson, by his agent Alex. Richardson, has loaned to John Lyon three hundred and fifty dollars and Lyon has deposited with Alex Richardson as agent for Henderson, a negro boy slave named Dave, about 16 years old to work and labor for the use of said money, until next July when Lyon is to return the money aand said negro to be returned. 7 Feb. 1815   Alex Richardson, agent for L. L. Henderson   John Lyon   Teste: James Head
– May Term 1815 This Article of Agreement proved by the oath of James Head and ordered to be registered. [p258]
Sum of one hundred and fifty dollars paid me by L. L. Henderson by A. Richardson, his agent, I convey to Henderson said negro Dave. 6 July 1816 John Lyon   Teste: J. Trimble, Jas. Langley
- July Sessions 1816 This transfer on the back of Article of Agreement was proven by the oath of James Langley and ordered registered. [p259]

DEADERICK, George M.   Bill of Sale   20 Sept 1816
I have sold to George M. Deaderick one negro man slave called Isaac, about thirty years of age, and lately the property of Burwell Quimby. 24 Nov. 1814
        E. Fitzhugh   Witness: Z. Cantrell
- January Sessions This bill of sale proved by the oath of Zebulan Cantrell and ordered to be registered. [p260]

DEADERICK, Geo. M.   Bill of Sale   20 Sept 1816
I have this day sold to George M. Deaderick one negro woman named Cate, about thirty two years - the same I lately purchased from John Raines.
15 Jan. 1816 E. Fitzhugh   Teste: Z. Cantrell
- January Sessions This bill of sale was proven by the oath of Zebulon Cantrell and ordered to be registered. [p261]

NEWNAN, John   Bill of Sale   20 Sept. 1816
I have sold to John Newnan fellow called Ben, about twenty five years of age.
7 Jan. 1815   John Nichols   Teste: Rich'd B. Owen
- July Sessions This bill of sale was proven by the oath of Richard B. Owen and ordered registered. [p262]

NEWNAN, John   Bill of Sale   20 Sept 1816
Sold this 13th day of January 1816 a negro fellow named Harry, about 28 years
of age, to J. Newnan. William Gleaves   Thomas Gleaves, Junior
Wit: R. B. Owen
- July Sessions   This bill of sale proven to be the act of the said William and
Thomas Gleaves by the oath of Richard B. Owen and ordered registered. [p263]

BECK, John E.   Bill of Sale   20 Sept 1816
I, Mary Beck, have sold to John B. Beck a negro man slave named Ceasar.
3 Jan. 1816   Mary Beck   Test: W. Barrow, Sarah E. Harris
- April Sessions This bill of sale was proven by the oath of Willie Barrow and
ordered registered. [p264]

HARTLEY & BENNING   Bill of Sale   20 Nov. 1816
We, John Bowden and John Robertson, have sold to Charles Harley and James
Benning a negro woman by the name of Mary and her child by the name of
Genny; the woman about 20 years old and her child about three months old. 5
Dec. 1815   John Bowden   John Robison   Teste: John W. Whitfield, A. Lard
- July Sessions   This bill of sale proven by the oath of John Whitfield and
ordered to be registered. [p265]

WHITE, Asa   Bill of Sale   2 December 1816
I, George W. Charlton, have sold to Asa White a certain yellow negro boy named
Sonne, about sixteen years old. 5 August 1816   George W. Charlton   Teste:
James Carter, Merry C. Abston
- October Sessions   This bill of sale was proven by the oath of James Carter
and Merry C. Abston and ordered to be registered. [p266]

CAMP, James [children of]   Bill of Sale   2 Dec. 1816
I, William B. Wood, have left with James Camp a negro girl, Emeline, which
negro girl is hereby transfered to his children and their heirs, upon this condition
however, if I am in any manner injured by being security for said James Camp
to the administration of Joseph Wood, dec'd on a bond given by said James
Camp on which I am security, I am to be indemnified by said negro. 7 Aug 1815
        William B. Wood   Teste: James Trimble
- This conditional bill of sale was proven by the oath of James Trimble, Esquire
and ordered to be registered. [p267]

PIERCE, Jeremiah   Bill of Sale   2 Dec. 1816
I, Henry J. Handly, of the County of Montgomery and State of Tennessee have
sold to Jeremiah Pierce one negro girl about eight years of age, named Rachael.
7 April 1816   Henry J. Handley   Teste: W. Wallace
- October Sessions   This bill of sale was proven by the oath of William Wallace

65

and ordered to be registered. [p268]

HANNAH, James   Bill of Sale   18 Dec. 1816
We have sold to James Hannah a negro man named Harry. 30 Dec. 1815
 Anderson Pride William Maxey, Admr.
Teste: Thos. Deaderick, Jno. Deatherage
- Nov. Term This bill of sale was proved by the oath of Thos. Deaderick and ordered to be registered. [p269]

WELLS, E.   Bill of Sale   2 Jan. 1816
I have this day sold a negro man named Randol to John Page, said negro is not more than twenty three years old. 9 July 1814 E. Wells Teste: C. Stump
- May Term This bill of sale was proven by the oath of C. Stump and ordered registered. [p270]

MORGAN, Wm C.   Bill of Sale   9 Jan. 1817
I do sell to William C. Morgan my full and exclusive right and life estate, it being all the right I have to the following negroes: Sandy, a negro man about thirty years of age; Saluda, a girl about six years old. 9 Feb. 1816 B. Seawell
Teste: M. H. Quinn, Tho. S. King
- April Sessions This bill of sale acknowledged by Benjamin Seawell to be his act and ordered registered. [p271]

KING, Tho. S.   Bill of Sale   9 Jan. 1817
I sell to Thomas S. King my full and exclusive right and life estate, it being all the right I have, to the following negroes: Betty, a negro woman about forty years of age and Temperance, her daughter, about three years of age; also Mary, another of her children about two years of age. 9 Feb. 1816 B. Seawell
Teste: M. H. Quinn, Wm C. Morgan
- April Sessions This bill of sale acknowledged to be his act by the said Benjamin Seawell and ordered to be registered. [p272]

SEAWELL, Peggy Freer   Bill of Sale   9 Jan. 1817
I have sold my full right and life estate in and to the following property: one negro boy named George, about sixteen years old, also Billy, a boy ten years old and Jenny, a woman fifty years of age, to Peggy Freer Seawell. 9 Feb. 1816
   B. Seawell Teste: Tho. S. King
- April Sessions This bill of sale acknowledged by the said Benjamin Seawell and ordered to be registered. [p273]

BOSLEY, Beal   Bill of Sale   . 5 Feb. 1817
I, James Fox, have sold to Beal Bosley a negro boy of a yellow complexion, about thirteen years old, named Tom. 29 Jan. 1817 James Fox

- January Sessions This bill of sale was acknowledged by the said James Fox to be his act and deed and ordered registered. [p274]

SEARCY, Robert   Bill of Sale   5 Feb. 1817
I, Jesse Wharton, administrator to the estate of William Wharton, have sold to Robert Searcy a negro boy about fifteen years old, who is called and known by the name of Parlor of mixed blood; viz Black & White, is unfortunately a slave for life. 19 Nov. 1816 J. Wharton   Teste: S. Cantrell, Jr.
- January Sessions This bill of sale was acknowledged by the said Jesse Wharton, Admr. and ordered to be registered. [p275]

BASS, Thos. S.   Bill of Sale   5 Feb. 1817
Thomas Jones, of Giles county, for divers good reasons, considering him moving, has this day sold to Thomas S. Bass, of Davidson county, all the title and claim to a deed of gift made on 7 March 1810 by John Bass to him, he has to the following negroes; Moses, Austin & Nelson, to use & enjoy the right & title by this indenture conveyed. 16 Jan. 1817   Thos. Jones
Teste: A. V. Brown , F. Sanders
- January Sessions This bill of sale was proven by the oath of Aaron V. Brown and Fayette Sanders and ordered to be registered. [p276]

McFADDEN, Candour   Bill of Sale   7 Feb. 1817
Received payment in full from Cander McFadden for a negro man slave named Cuff, aged about twenty years. 27 Sept. 1815 Enoch Ensley
Teste: Ralph Blair, William P. Seat
- January Sessions This Bill of Sale was acknowledged by the said Enoch Ensley to be his act and ordered to be registered. [p277]

TALLY, Nelson   Bill of Sale   7 Feb. 1817
I, Robert S. Harris, of the county of Giles, have sold unto Nelson Tally of the county of Davidson a certain negro woman named Eady supposed to be twenty eight years of age. 9 Sept 1816 Robert S. Harris
Teste: W. Wisenor, E. Pritchett
- January Sessions   This Bill of Sale was proven by the oath of William Wisenor and Ephraim Pritchett and ordered to be registered. [p278]

LIDDON, William A. & Benjamin F.   Bill of Sale   7 February 1817
I, Samuel Weakley, have sold to William A. Lidden and Benjamin F. Lidden, a negro boy named Alexander, supposed to be six or seven years old, which said negro boy was levied on and sold by Michael C. Dunn, Sheriff of Davidson County as the property of William T. Henderson and conveyed by Dunn to Weakley by bill of sale bearing date 14 Feb. 1815.
31 Jan. 1817 Sam'l Weakley

- January Sessions This bill of sale was acknowledged by Samuel Weakley to be his act and ordered to be registered. [p279]

WILLIAMS, Will   Mortgage   7 February 1817
I have sold to Will Williams a negro man named Jerry about thirty six years of age, redeemable however by payment of the debt within six months.
6 January 1817 Dougless Purkett   Wit: J. F. Williams, Jno Drewry
- January Sessions This Bill of Sale with redemption was proven by the oaths of Josiah F. Williams and John Drury and ordered to be registered. [p280]

JOSLIN, Daniel   Bill of Sale   15 May 1817
I, Williamson Harper, have sold unto Daniel Joslin a negro girl named Tenessee, about four years old. 30 Jan. 1817   William (X) Harper
Teste: Jessee Newlan, Fr. Machershead, James Baxter
- April Sessions This bill of sale was acknowledged by Williamson Harper to be his act and ordered to be registered. [p281]

HOOPER, Nimrod   Bill of Sale   15 May 1817
I, Douglass Puckett, have sold to Nimrod Hooper a negro man slave named Jerry, about the age of thirty seven. 1 April 1817   Douglass Puckett
Teste: Will Williams, Stephen C. McDaniel
-April Sessions This bill of sale proved by the oath of William Williams and Stephen C. McDaniel. [p282]

RUTHERFORD, Wm   Bill of Sale with Redemption   19 May 1817
I, William Rutherford, have sold to McKiernan & Stout a negro boy slave named Arthur, about fourteen years of age; if debt is paid, this deed to be void.
15 Feb. 1817 Wm Rutherford   Teste: Robt. P. Dunlop, Ephraim H. Foster
- April Sessions This Bill of Sale with redemption was proven by the oaths of Robert P. Dunlop and Ephraim H. Foster and ordered to be registered. [p284]

SEAT, William P.   Bill of Sale   19 May 1817
We have sold to William P. Seat a negro girl named Elsa. 24 Sept. 1816
J. W. Glasgow J. Glasgow   Teste Moses Christenberry Godfry Shelton
- April Sessions This Bill of Sale - James W. Glasgow and James Glasgow to William P. Seat was proven by the oath of Moses Christenberry and Godfry Shelton and ordered registered. [p284]

TALLY, Nelson   Bill of Sale   19 Aug. 1817
I, Robert S. Harris, of Giles County, State of Tennessee have sold to Nelson Tally a negro boy named George. 27 Jan. 1817   Robert S. Harris
Witness: Landon C. Farrar William Harris
- July Sessions This bill of sale was proven by the oaths of Landon Farror &

William Harris and ordered to be registered. [p285]

LOFTIN, Thomas   Bill of Sale   19 Aug. 1817
I, Thomas Loftin, sell unto Williamson Loftin one negro boy named Valentine,
about six years old.20 March 1815   Thomas Loftin
Teste: Jno Davis   Robert Simpson
 - Jan. Sessions 1816 This bill of sale proven by the oath of John Davis and
ordered to be certified. [p286]
 - July Sessions 1817   This bill of sale was proven by the oath of Robert
Simpson & ordered registered. [p286]

SANDERS, Francis   Bill of Sale   19 Aug 1817
I, Lemuel Kennedy, have sold to Francis Sanders a negro boy named Joseph of
the age of twelve years. 1 July 1817   Lemuel Kennedy
Teste: William Matlock Jesse Cutler
 - July Sessions This bill of sale was proven by the oath of Jesse Cutler and
ordered registered. [p287]

GREENE, Robert W.   Bill of Sale   20 Aug 1817
I, Edmond Owen, have sold to Robert W. Greene a negro man slave named
Samuel, about twenty one years of age. 29 July 1817   Edmund Owen
Teste: Tho Childress Ethelbert Sanders
 - July Sessions This bill of sale was acknowledged by Edmund Owen to be his
act and ordered to be registered. [p288]

SANDERS, Francis   Bill of Sale   20 Aug 1817
I, Lemuel Kennedy, have sold to Francis Sanders a negro boy named Aron, aged
twelve years. 11 June 1817   Lem'l Kennedy
 Witness: William Matlock Jesse Cutler
 - July Sessions This bill of sale was proven by the oath of William Matlock and
Jesse Cutler and ordered to be registered. [p289]

COCKRILL, John   Bill of Sale   26 Aug 1817
I, John Johnson of Williamson county and State of Tennessee, have sold to John
Cockrill one negro woman named Pheobe. 7 March 1817   John Johnson
Teste: Carban Noles Lucy (X) Noles
 - August Sessions This bill of sale was proven by the oath of Carban Noles and
Lucy Noles and ordered registered. [p290]

WHITESIDE, Jenkin   Bill of Sale   16 October 1817
I, Ernest Benoit, have sold J. Whiteside one female negro slave named Phebe,
about twenty five years of age. 15 March 1817   Ernest Benoit
Teste: Wm Quarles

- May Sessions This bill of sale was acknowledged by Ernest Benoit and ordered to be registered. [p291]

FLOURNAY, Silas   Deed of Relinquishment   11 Nov. 1817
I, Silas Flournay of the County of Giles and State of Tennessee, has this day relinquished my title and claim to a negro boy named Cyrus unto John Nichol of Nashville; aforesaid boy having been conveyed by John Cannon to John Nichol the 1st of August 1814 at Lexington, KY, and the sale ratified by William Cannon, Sr., the 12th August the same year. 13 August 1817 Silas Flournoy
Witness: James C. Rooker   James D. Murry
- October Sessions This Deed of Relinquishment was acknowledged by the said Silas Flournoy and ordered registered. [p292]

BOOTH, Robert   Bill of Sale   11 Nov 1817
I, Henry Booth, sell to Robert Booth all the title, claim and interest I hold in a certain negro boy named Jacob, willed to myself & William Booth after the death of Andrew Boothe, for whose benefit the negro is for, agreeable to the will of Henry Boothe, dec'd. 8 Jan 1816 Henry Boothe
Teste: Jhn Coates   Greenwood Payne
- July Sessions 1816 This bill of sale proven by the oath of Greenwood Payne and ordered registered. [p293]

OWEN, Edmond   Bill of Sale   11 Nov 1817
I, Lee Wilson, have sold to Edmond Owen a negro man about twenty five years old named Prush. 18 August 1817 Lee Wilson Wit: H. Greene Tho Childress
- This bill of sale was proven by the oath of Horrace Greene and Thomas Childress and ordered registered. [p294]

HANKS, Richard   Bill of Sale   14 Nov 1817
I, T. W. Gilmon, have sold unto Richard Hanks a parcel of household furniture (to wit) one Set of Madison Tables, one Set of green chairs, one Set of first Wale chairs, which is now at Williams in Nashville and Sekatary and Book Cases which is now at General Carrolls brick house, formerly owned by Edmond D. Hobby, 20 Oct 1817 Timothy W. Gilman Teste Wm W. Goodwin
- October Sessions This bill of sale proved by the oath of Wm W. Goodwin and ordered to be registered. [pp295]

CANTRELL, Stephen, Jr.   Bill of Sale   29 Nov. 1817
I, Jlai Metcalf, have sold to Stephen Cantrell, Jr. & David Irwin a negro man slave named Major, a bricklayer & stone mason by trade, now in the employ of Lewis White. 1 May 1817 Jlai Metcalf   Wit: L. Spain Geo Shall
- October Sessions This bill of sale proved by the oath of George Shall and ordered to be registered. [p296]

FITZHUGH, Samuel   Bill of Sale   13 Dec. 1817
I, John Mayfield, have sold to Samuel Fitzhugh two negro slaves, Sarah and
Amanda, a girl child of Sarah. 21 August 1815   John Mayfield
Teste: James Fitzhugh William Lemonds
 - Davidson Circuit Court May term 1817 This bill of sale was acknowledged
by the said Jno Mayfield and ordered to be registered. [p297]

PORTER, Alex   Bill of Sale   21 Jan'y 1818
I, Thos. B. Smith of Rutherford Co., have this day sold to Alex. Porter a negro
man named Jacob, a carpenter, about thirty years of age. 17 July 1817
   Tho. B. Smith   Teste: Fra's May John Spence, Jr.
 - Davidson Circuit Court Nov. Term 1817 This bill of sale was proven by the
oath of John Spence, and Wm Lytle made oath that he is acquainted with the
handwriting of Francis May, the other subscribing witness, and that he believes
the signature of the said Francis May to be in the proper handwriting and that the
said Francis May is dead; ordered to be registered. [p298]

McGAVOCK, James   Bill of Sale   18 Feb. 1818
I, Alfred Nichols, have this day sold to James McGavock a negro boy slave
named Harry, about fourteen years of age. 24 Jan. 1818 A. Nichols
 Teste: C. L. Byrn
 - January Session This bill of sale was proven by the oath of Charles L. Byrn
and ordered to be registered. [p299]

BENOIT, E.   Bill of Sale   18 Feb. 1818
We, Thomas Ransey and Robert Greene, have sold to Ernest Benoit a negro man
named Harry. 18 Jan. 1814   Thomas Ramsey Rob: W. Greene
 Teste Wm Thompson W. Hayner
 - January Session This bill of sale was acknowledged by the said Thomas &
Robert W. to be their act and ordered to be registered. [p300]

DEADERICK, George M.   Bill of Sale   18 Feb. 1818
I, Bennet Searcy, have sold to George M. Deaderick the following negroes;
Philis, about thirty years; Anthony, aged about six years; Milly, aged about three
years; Harriatt, aged about one year old. 3 Feb. 1812   B. Searcy
Teste: Stephen Cantrell, Jr.   Tho. J. Read
 - January Session This bill of sale was proven by the oath of Thomas J. Read
and ordered to be registered. [p301]

SEARCY, R. & CANTRELL, S., Jr.   Deed of Trust   18 Feb. 1818
George M. Deaderick, for the love and affection he bears for Marcia F. Searcy,
daughter of Bennet Searcy, sell & convey to Stephen Cantrell, Jr. and Robert
Searcy, in trust for the said Marcia F. Searcy, the three following negroes; a boy

named Anthony, about six years of age; a girl named Milly, about three years of age; a girl named Harriatt, about one year old, all the children of a negro woman named Phillis, lately the property of the said Bennet Searcy; to the use of Bennet Searcy and Mary, his wife, during their natural lives, and at the death of the said Bennet and Mary, the aforesaid three negroes and their increase I hereby set over to the said Stephen Cantrell and Robert Searcy in trust for the sole use and benefit of her, the said Marcia F. Searcy, her heirs and assigns forever.
5 June 1812   George M. Deaderick   Wits: J. Childress   Duncan Robertson
- Jan'y Session This bill of sale was proven by the oath of Duncan Robertson and ordered to be registered. [p303]

EASTLAND, Thos.   Bill of Sale   20 March 1818
I, John A. Eastland, have sold unto Thomas Eastland two negroes; Sally Gibson, a woman aged about twenty four and Daniel, her son, aged about six years. 25 Jan. 1817 John A. Eastland   Teste: Jewett F. Fletcher Daniel McGonegall
- October Session This bill of sale was proven by the oath of Daniel McGonegall and Jewet F. Fletcher and ordered to be registered. [p304]

EASTLAND, Thos.   Bill of Sale   20 March 1818
We, Jos. Philip, shff of Davidson County, by John F. Dismuke, his Deputy of the one part and Tho. Eastland. Hereby sell to Thos Eastland a billiard table and a negro woman named Sally Gibson, purchased by James Telford and by him ordered to be transferred to Thomas Eastland which property was sold and the property of John A. Eastland. 13 Oct. 1817
Jos. Philips, Shff by John F. Dismukes, Dp
- October Session This bill of sale was acknowledged by John F. Dismukes, Deputy and ordered to be registered. [p305]

WHITESIDE, J.   Bill of Sale   24 March 1818
I, Joseph Philips, Esqr., Sheriff of Davidson County by John F. Dismukes, my Deputy by virtue of two writs; one Joseph & Robert Woods against William Rutherford, the other Thomas J. Bradford against said Rutherford seized sundry articles of personal property and among others one chestnut sorrell horse, about nine years old; one bright sorrell colt, two years old; one bright sorrel filly rising two years old; one spotted cow & her calf and one brindle cow without horns, and her calf, one dunn cow with a bell; four feather beds with the bedstead & furniture, one cupboard, one bureau, one buffet with its contents, one chest, one trunk and all the other household furniture of said William Rutherford, then in his house, one coffeemill, one oven, two pots and all the other kitchen furniture and I, Joseph Philips, by said John F. Dismukes, my Deputy on the 4th day of November in the year aforesaid, at the dwelling house of said William Rutherford, exposed to public sale the personal property so seized and then and there sold to Jenkin Whiteside being the last and highest bidder.

29 December 1817   Joseph Phillips, Shff
- January Sessions This Indenture of bargain and sale was acknowledged by the
said Joseph Philips, Sheriff and ordered to be registered. [pp307/308]

CLAIBORNE, Thos.   Bill of Sale   25 March 1818
I, William Rutherford, have sold to Thomas Claiborne eight negro slaves; Will,
an old man of very black color whose age is unknown; Patt, a negro woman,
about twenty five years, her child Simon, about two years old, also her child
Sinda, about twelve months; Delphy, a girl about eight years, Ephraim, a boy
about six; Jerry, a boy about three years old and Hiram, a boy about two years
old. 21 October 1817 Wm Rutherford   Teste: Sam'l Weakley   J. Gordon
- I, Thomas Claiborne, set over to J. Whiteside all my right and title to the
within eight negroes. 3 Nov. 1817   Th. Claiborne
Teste: John F. Dismukes   T. G. Bradford
- January Sessions This Bill of Sale was acknowledged by William Rutherford
and also proven by the oath of James Gordon and on the back of said bill of sale
is a transfer of said slaves to Jenkin Whitesides dated 3 Nov. 181, and proven
by the oath of John S. Dismukes and Thomas G. Bradford & ordered to be
registered. [pp308/309/310]

COCKRILL, John, Jr.   Bill of Sale   27 March 1818
I, Alexander W. Jones, have this day sold to John Cockrill, Jr. the following
negroes; Sandy, Abraham, Ginney, Emanuel, Daniel and Selina; seven head
horses and ten head of cattle and all my household furniture. and also bind myself
to make and convey a title to one hundred acres of land in Wilson County.
25 Feb. 1818 Alex'r W. Jones   Teste: Wm P. Strike Moses F. Roberts
- March Term   4th Judicial Circuit This bill of sale was proven by the oath
of Moses F. Roberts and the said Roberts also made oath that he saw William P.
Strike sign his name thereto as a witness and he was informed by the said
witness Strike, that he resided out of this State, to wit in the City of Baltimore.
[pp310/311]

BARROW, M.   Bill of Sale   27 March 1818
I, John Cockrill, Jr. of the County of Bedford and State of Tennessee, have this
day sold to Matthew Barrow, payment being a note of Alex'r W. Jones, a sorrell
horse about eight years old, said horse was sold by James Camp to Alex'r W.
Jones and from said Jones to the said John Cockrill, Jr. 16 March 1818
J. Cockrill   Attese: William Thomas Dickinson   Was. L. Hannum
- 4th Judicial Circuit March Term This bill of sale was proven by the oath of
Washington L. Hannum. [p312]

HART, William   Bill of Sale   18 April 1818
I, John Cockrill, Junr, of Bedford County, have sold to William Hart the

73

following negro slaves: Abram, about thirty five years of age and Sandy about twenty seven years of age which said negroes were sold by Alexander Jones to the said John Cockrill, Junr. 17 March 1818   J. Cockrill
Teste: E. Pritchett   Richard Watkins
- 4th Judicial Circuit March Term   This bill of sale was proven by the oaths of E. Pritchett and Richard Watkins and ordered to be certified for registration. [p313]

HART, William   Bill of Sale   18 March 1818
I, Alexander Jones, have sold to William Hart a certain negro girl slave named Emeline, daughter of Patt and allotted to me in the late division of my fathers estate. 26 March 1818   Alex Jones   Teste: Jno. McLemore   J. Blackfan
- 4th Judicial Circuit March Term This bill of sale was proven by the oaths of John C. McLemore and J. Blackfan and ordered to be registered. [p314]

DARBY & CRAIGHEAD   Power of Attorney   21 April 1818
I, Robert J. Nelson of Maury County and State of Tennessee, possessing full faith and confidence in the ability and integrity of David Craighead, Esqr & Patrick H. Darby, Esqr., do appoint them joint and several attorneys in fact for me to sell and transfer my title and claim to the following property: one tract of 640 acres of land on Yellow Creek in Dickson or Montgomery County and half of a 640 acre tract of land on Cumberland River in Montgomery County and 274 acre tract in said last mentioned county joining Mr. Northinglan, 274 acres in Maury County on Duck River granted to Thomas Shute, also can draw any warrants for land belonging to me and act as my agents in the same manner as if it was done by me. 13 Sept 1817   Robert J. Nelson
Teste: David Campbell John Walker John T. Dismukes Wm Donnison
- 4th Circuit Court This Power of Attorney was proven by the oaths of Jno T. Dismukes and Wm Donnison and ordered to be registered. [pp315/316]

JONES, Alex'r W.   Bill of Sale   25 April 1818
I, John Cockrill, Jr., of the county of Bedford and State of Tennessee, have this day sold to Matthew Barrow one sorrell horse about eight years old, said horse was sold by James Camp to Alex W. Jones and by said Jones to the said John Cockrill, Jr. 16 March 1818
I, Alexander W. Jones , confirm the aforesaid sale. 27 March 1818 A. W. Jones   Wit: Donald Fraser E. L. Hall
- April Sessions   This bill of sale was proven by the oaths of Donald Frazer and Elisha L. Hall. [pp316/317]

PEARCE, Jeremiah   Bill of Sale   29 May 1818
We, Stump and Cox, have this day sold to Jeremiah Pearce one negro woman by the name of Juday, aged about twenty six years that said Stump bought of Chin..

74

14 August 1816   Stump & Cox   Teste: B. Laneir Peberson (X) Vader
- April Sessions   This bill of sale was acknowledged by John Stump and ordered to be registered. [p318]

PAGE, Vinson   Bill of Sale   7 August 1818
I, John Page, have this day sold unto Vinson Page the following property: one negro boy by the name of Mike, aged twelve years old; one negro boy by the name of Charles, aged ten; one negro girl named Tildy, aged eight; one negro boy named Jurd, aged six; one negro boy named Henry, aged four; one negro girl named Charlot, aged two. 23 July 1818   John (X) Page
Teste: W. Wallace Stephen Johnston
- July Session This bill of sale was proven by the oaths of William Wallace and Stephen Johnston and ordered to be registered. [p319]

WINSTEAD, Lucy Ann   Bill of Sale   7 August 1818
I, William Winstead, sell to Lucy Ann Winstead, her heirs and assigns three negroes; Milley, about twenty years old; Esther, about four years old and Caroline, about sixteen months old; also two featherbeds and furniture, one Bureau, one Cupboard and the furniture in it, one sugar chest, one folding table, two womens saddles & bridles, one mans saddle, one looking glass, a quantity of bacon, a quantity of wheat & corn, also all my crop of grain, tobacco etc. for the year, also all the fowls belonging to the farm. 22 April 1818   Wm Winstead
Wits: Lucy Smith   Henry (X) Cartwright Seth Davis Joseph Prichard
- July Session This bill of sale was acknowledged by the said William Winstead and ordered to be registered. [p320]

WINSTEAD, Samuel   Bill of Sale   8 August 1818
I, William Winstead, have sold to Samuel Winstead, of the County of Williamson, one waggon and gears, five head of horses, twenty one head of cattle, eighteen head of sheep, sixty five head of hoggs, two featherbeds and furniture, two chests and three trunks, one cupboard & furniture, one dozen chairs, one shot gunn, one loom, three washing tubs, six pails and piggins, four pots, one large kettle, two ovens, four skillets, one iron fire stick, one pair of tongs and shovel, one pair of fire dogs, one pair flat irons, one tea kettle, one pair waffle iron, a quantity of flax and cotton. 25 April 1818   Wm Winstead
Witness: Guy Smith, Henry (X) Cartwright, Seth Davis, Joseph Prichard
- Jualy Sessions This bill of sale was acknowledged by the said William Winstead & ordered to be registered. [p321]

HOOPER, Nimrod   Bill of Sale   8 August 1818
I, Nimrod Hooper, have sold to Lewis Earthman one negro boy by the name of Bill, aged fourteen. 19 Nov. 1814   Nimrod Hooper
Teste: A. Hooper Thomas Marrys

- July Sessions This bill of sale was proven by the oath of Absalam Hooper and ordered to be so certified. [p322]

PHILIPS, JOSEPH   Bill of Sale   8 August 1818
I, William Thos. Dickinson, have sold to Joseph Philips nine negro slaves: Bob, about twenty one years of age; Mitchel, a man about nineteen years of age; Cate, about forty five years old; Cloe, about eight years old; Flora, about seventeen years old; Aggy about sixteen years old; Mary, about ten years old; Ben about four years old and Peter about one year old. 22 Dec. 1817
   William Thomas Dickinson   Teste: Duke W. Sumner, Jacob Dickinson
- July Sessions This bill of sale was proven by the oath of Jacob Dickinson and ordered to be certified. [p323]

PAGE, Vinson   Bill of Sale   10 August 1818
I, John Page, have sold to Vinson Page the following property: two feather beds and bedsteads and furniture, household and kitchen furniture and plantation working tools and also the present crop of corn growing and two hundred weights of bacon, six head of horses, six head of cattle, six head of sheep, twenty head of hoggs. 28 July 1818   John (X) Page   Teste: W. Wallace, Jas. Lovell
- July Sessions This bill of sale was proven by the oaths of William Wallace and James Lovell and ordered to be registered. [p324]

GREENE, R. W.   Bill of Sale   10 August 1818
I, Francis McKay, have sold to R. W. Greene one negro boy named John. 17 June 1818   Francis McKay   Teste: Jo. H. Greene
- July Sessions This bill of sale was proven by the oath of Jo. H. Green and ordered to be registered. [p325]

ARTHUR, William   Bill of Sale   10 August 1818
I, James Buck, convey to William Arthur all the personal property in the attached schedule as my security to the house of Marshall and Watkins of Nashville: 1 bed, bedstead & furniture, one china press & furniture, one bureau, one dining table, one bedstead & furniture, one mattress and furniture, one bedstead, one sugar chest, sundry kitchen furniture, six chairs, 3 common chairs, one cradle, two pair irons, 2 cows, 3 glass jars, 3 stone jars, 4 tumblers, 2 decanters, 3 trunks, 2 smoothing irons, 2 small tables, 7 pitchers, one writing desk, 3 doz. lashes, 5 shoemaking benches, 2 pr boot trees. 9 June 1818
James (X) Buck   Teste: Young D. Davis
- July Sessions This bill of sale was proven by the oath of Young D. Davis and ordered registered. [pp326/327]

REDING, Iredell   Bill of Sale   29 Sept. 1818
I, Call McNeill, have sold to Iredell Reding a certain negro woman called Jude,

twenty two years of age.

28 July 1817   Call McNeill   Teste: Daniel Buie, Shaderich Rawley
- October Sessions This bill of sale was acknowledged by Call McNeill and ordered registered. [p328]

McMURRY, Wm   Bill of Sale   30 Sept. 1818
Whereas a Writ was issued from the County Court of Davidson on the goods and chattels of Floyd Hurt at the instance of Timothy Guard and Jos. Philips, sheriff by John F. Dismukes, his Deputy, did levy on a negro boy named Fortune, aged fourteen years and said boy Fortune was offered for sale on Saturday, 18th of Oct. and was purchased by Robert Wood and by order from Wood the bill of sale is made to William McMurry. 18 October 1817
Jos. Philips, Sheff by John F. Dismukes, Dep.
- October Sessions 1817 This bill of sale was acknowledged by John F. Dismukes, Deputy Sheriff and ordered to be registered. [p329]

BOYD, Richard   Bill of Sale   12 Nov. 1818
I, Josiah Horton, have sold to Richard Boyd one negro woman, aged twenty seven, named Fanny, also her boy child named Luke, better than two years old.
8 Sept. 1818   J. Horton
- October Sessions This bill of sale was acknowledged by Josiah Horton and ordered registered. [p330]

DUPREE, Nancy & children   Covenant   12 Nov. 1818
Whereas James Dupree and Nancy Dupree, his wife, have conveyed to M. Barrow and others all the right, title & interest unto one land warrant located at the Mouth of Hatchey River on the Mississippi River in the name of John Nichols; the sum received for the sale of the warrant shall be paid to Archibald Lytle, Jr. the for the use benefit of Nancy Dupree and her children and the same to apply to the education of the children aforesaid that now are, or may be, by the said Nancy Dupree. Said Lytle to be at the trouble without fee or reward. 19 October 1818   Archibald Lytle   Teste: M. Barrow
- October Sessions This Covenant was proven by the oath of Matthew Barrow and ordered registered.
[pp 330/331]

HARDGRAVE, John & Skelton   Bill of Sale   12 Nov. 1818
I, Francis Hardgrave, have sold to John and Skelton Hardgrave a negro man named Stephen. 19 October 1818   Francis Hardgrave
Teste: Thomas Demoss, B. F. Robertson
- October Sessions This bill of sale was proven by the oath of Thomas Demoss and Benjamin F. Robertson and ordered registered. [p331]

HARDGRAVE, John & Skelton   Bill of Sale   12 Nov. 1818
I, Francis Hardgrave, have sold to John and Skelton Hardgrave a negro boy
named Green. 8 April 1818   Francis Hardgrave
Teste: John Demoss, Thomas Loftin
 - October Sessions This bill of sale was proven by the oath of John Demoss and
Thomas Loftin and ordered registered. [p332]

HARDGRAVE, John & Skelton   Bill of Sale   12 Nov. 1818
I, Francis Hardgrave, have sold to John and Skelton Hardgrave seven negro
slaves named Phillis, Jurdon, Darkcus, Allen, Claborne, Colman, & Charles. 7
April 1818   Francis Hardgrave   Teste: Thomas Demoss, Thomas Loftin
 - October Sessions   This bill of sale was proven by the oath of Thomas
Demoss and Thomas Loftin and ordered registered. [pp331/332]

TELFORD, Samuel   Bill of Sale   12 Nov. 1818
I, John Johns of the County of Rutherford, have delivered to Samuel Telford one
negro slave, Nancy, about twenty years old. 21 October 1818   A. Johns as
agent for John Johns   Teste: C. Stump
 - October Sessions This bill of sale was acknowledged by John Johns by his
agent, A. Johns, and ordered registered. [p333]

HOOPER, Nimrod   Bill of Sale   12 Nov. 1818
I, John McMurrien of Putnam County in the State of Georgia, have sold to
Nimrod Hooper a mulatto boy between fifteen and sixteen years, named Billey.
27 July 1814   John McMurrien Wit: James Moses
 - October Sessions This bill of sale was proven by the oath of James Moses and
ordered registered. [p334]

McCLELLAND, Catherine   Bill of Sale   12 Nov. 1818
I, Thomas Williamson, in consideration of the natural love and affection which
I bare to my daughter, Catherine McClelland of the County of Williamson, and
in consideration of one dollar to me in hand paid by the said Catherine grant unto
the said Catherine McClellan, her heirs, executors, administrators and assigns,
one mulatto girl by the name of Amy, about the age of sixteen years; also one
negro boy by the name of Green, about the age of two years and six months old.
20 October 1818 Thomas Williamson   Teste: James D. Williamson
 - October Sessions This bill of sale was acknowledged by Thomas Williamson
and ordered to be registered. [pp334/335]

McGAVOCK, David   Bill of Sale   12 Nov. 1818
I, James Lovell, only acting executor of the last will and testament of William
Grimes, late of the county of Davidson and State of Tennessee, Deceased , and
as Attorney in fact for all the heirs of the said William Grimes have this day in

open markets by Duncan Robertson, Auctioneer, sold to David McGavock a negro woman named Fanny, about twenty two years of age and her son Thomas, a mulatto slave six years old. 26 Sept. 1818 Jas. Lovell
Teste: M. C. Dunn, F. McGavock
 - October Sessions This bill of sale was proven by the oath of M. C. Dunn and Francis McGavock and ordered registered. [pp335/336]

WILLIAMSON, Sarah   Bill of Sale   12 Nov. 1818
I, Thomas Williamson, for and in consideration of the natural love and affection I bare to my daughter, Sarah Williamson and in further consideration of one dollar to me in hand paid by the said Sarah, grant unto the said Sarah, her heirs, executors, administrators and assigns one negro girl by the name of Susan, about thirteen years of age and also one negro boy by the name of Will, about the age of six years. 20 Oct. 1818 Thomas Williamson   Wit: James D. Williamson
 - October Sessions This bill of sale was acknowledged by Thomas Williamson and ordered to be registered. [pp336/337]

PORTER, George   Bill of Sale   22 March 1819
I, John Keys, have sold to George Porter a negro woman by the name of Milley. 14 April 1818   John Keys   Teste: Lewis Speice, John Moore
 - January Sessions 1819   This bill of sale was proven by the oath of Lewis Speice and John Moore and ordered registered. [p337]

TALLEY, Nelson   Bill of Sale   22 March 1819
I, Willie Barrow, have sold unto Nelson Talley one negro fellow named Eamond, about thirty three years of age, not guaranteed as sound as it is well known to both parties that he is affected with a rupture in his groin supposed occasioned by lifting. 19 Jan 1819 M. Barrow Wit: Ebanezer Titus, Ken-- t Well
 - January Sessions This bill of sale was acknowledged by Willie Barrow and ordered registered. [pp337/338]

MATHIAS, Mary   Bill of Sale   22 March 1819
I have sold to Mary Mathias and her heirs a negro woman named Jemima and her child Caroline. 13 March 1811   Finch Scruggs   Teste: Thomas Patteson
 - Jan'y Sessions This bill of sale was proven by the oath of Thomas Patteson and ordered to be registered. [p338]

PRYOR, Nicholas B.   Bill of Sale   22 March 1819
I, Joshua P. Vaughn, administrator of the estate of Thomas Williams, deceased, have sold to Nicholas B. Pryor a negro man named Edmund, about nineteen years of age. 23 Jan. 1819
          J. P. Vaughn, Admr of the estate of Thomas Williams, deceased
Wit: John Woodcock, J.... Curry

- January Sessions This bill of sale was proven by the oath of John Woodcock and J. Currey and ordered to be registered. [pp338/339]

ROBERTSON, John McNairy   Bill of Sale   22 March 1819
We, Levinea Beck, extrx, and Felix Robertson, Extr. of Jno. E. Beck, deceased have sold to John McNairy Robertson a negro man slave named Abram, about twenty four years of age, of black complexion. 7 Jan. 1819
     Levinia Beck   Felix Robertson   Teste: Th. Hill
- January Sessions This bill of sale was proved by the oath of Thomas Hill and ordered registered. [p339]

CLAIBORNE & ROBERTSON   Bill of Sale   23 March 1819
I, John C. Hicks, have sold to Thomas Claiborne and Felix Robertson the following negro slaves: Dinah, a yellow girl about twelve years of age; Betty, a girl about five years of age; Randall, a boy about four years of age. 15 July 1818
     Jno. C. Hicks   Teste: Th. Hill, Benj. F. Robertson
- July Sessions This bill of sale was proven by the oath of Thomas Hill and Benjamin F. Robertson and ordered to be registered. [p3440]

McIVER, John   Power of Attorney   23 March 1819
I, George W. Campbell, do hereby constitute and appoint John McIver of the County of Fairfax and Commonwealth of Virginia as my true and lawful attorney during my absence from the United States, to transact and manage my affairs in the State of Tennessee as well as renting and leasing my lands, collecting, receiving and paying monies due to or from me and to conduct my business in the Nashville Bank and in the Branch Bank of the State of Tennessee at Nashville and to rent or lease my house and lands in and near Nashville and to hire and take care of my slaves left there. 20 May 1818   G. M. Campbell
Teste: Tho. Crutcher, Robt H. Adams
- January Sessions This power of attorney was proven by the oath of Thomas Crutcher and Robert H. Adams and certified for registration. [pp340/341]

CHILDRESS, Edwin H.   Bill of Sale   31 March 1819
I, William Childress of Madison County in the Mississippi Territory sell to Edwin H. Childress of said County and Territory all my share, interest and claim to which I may be entitled by the last will and testament of my deceased Father after the death of my Stepmother, whether it be in negroes, household furniture or stock. 29 April 1817   Wm Childress
Teste: Sam'l Cruse, James G. Carroll
- Alabama Territory of the United States   At a County Court held for Madison County at the Courthouse in Huntsville on 28 Dec. 1818 this Deed from William Childress to Edwin H. Childress was produced and proved by the oaths of Samuel Cruse and James G. Carrel and ordered to be certified.

I, Henry Minor, Clerk of the County Court of Madison County certify that this deed is truly taken from the records of said Court. 4 Jan. 1819 Hy Minor, Clerk
I, Leroy Pope, Chief Justice and presiding magistrate, certify the foregoing. 4 Jan. 1819 [pp341/342/343]

COOPER, Edmond   Bill of Sale   31 March 1819
I have sold to Edmond Cooper a negro man slave by the name of Brister.
21 Jan. 1818   Jepthah Moseley   Test: L. Cooper
- This bill of sale was proven by the oath of L. Cooper and ordered registered. [p343]

SMITH, John H.   Bill of Sale   31 March 1819
I have this day sold and delivered to John H. Smith two negro slaves: Simon, about thirty five years old and Henrietta, about five years old. 12 Jan. 1819
J. R. Plummer   Teste: John Baird
- This bill of sale was proven by the oath of John Baird and ordered registered. [p343]

CANTRELL, HAMMUM & SEARCY   Deed of Trust   17 April 1819
Whereas John Stump and John S. Cox, merchants and partners in trade under the name of *Stump & Cox* are indebted to the Nashville Bank, Farmers & Mechanics Bank of Nashville, and to the Branch Bank of the State of Tennessee at Nashville ... whereas the contract entered into between John Stump on the one part and Robert Searcy, Stephen Cantrell and Washington L. Hammum on the other part ... the executors and administrators of the last survivor of them the following named negro slaves male and female: Nat, aged thirty seven; Tom, eighteen; Davey, thirty; Jim, twenty one; Big Toney, twenty one; Little Toney, twenty one; Jack, twenty seven; Isham twenty three; Daniel, seventeen; Dick, sixteen; George sixteen; Jacob, fifteen; Abram, nineteen; Drury, twenty three; Petmus, seventeen; Ben, sixteen; Isaac twelve; Little Tom, fourteen; Esther and her three children; Kate, twenty seven and her four children; Fanny, thirty; Daphney, twenty eight; Genney, twenty three and her two children; Clarissa, twenty five, and her three children; Letty, twenty seven and her two children; Milley, nineteen; Chloe, nineteen; Zedda, seventeen;' Till, fifteen; Phereby fifteen; Harriet, nineteen; Lizza, fourteen; Edmond twenty three; Ned twenty four; Sam, twenty six; George, twenty three; Harry, twenty six; Dick, twenty seven; Peyton, twenty three; March, twenty three; Gideon, nineteen; John, fifteen; Jacob, fifteen; Harry fourteen; Judy, twenty five; Nancy, twenty three; Milley, twenty three; Sarah, nineteen and her children; Lucy, twenty; Rossetta, twenty three; Lawsonberry, fifteen; Hanna, seven teen; Dina, fourteen and Zedda, twelve. 31 March 1819
John Stump Robert Searcy   Steph'n Cantrell   Was. L. Hammum
Teste: James Tilford, Wm Armstrong

- Supreme Court of Errors and Appeals for the fourth Circuit   March Term
This Deed of Trust was acknowledged by John Stump and Robert Searcy,
Stephen Cantrell and Washington L. Hammum and ordered registered. 1 April
1819 [pp344/345/346]

CRABB, Henry   Bill of Sale   19 May 1819
I, Charles L. Dibrell, sell to Henry Crabb a negro boy of a black colour, about
fourteen years old, named Harry. 23 March 1819   Chs. L. Dibrell
Teste: Nathan Ewing, Henry Ewing
- April Sessions This bill of sale was proven by the oath of Nathan Ewing and
Henry Ewing and ordered registered. [p347]

ALLEN, James   Bill of Sale   19 May 1819
Received of James Allen payment for a negro boy named Moses, about nine
months of age. 20 April 1819   David Allen   Teste: John Hall
- April sessions This bill of sale was acknowledged by David Allen and ordered
registered. [p347]

BUCHANAN, John   Bill of Sale   19 May 1819
I, Peter Simmerman of the County of Cumberland and State of Kentucky have
sold to John Buchanan a family of negroes: Exom, Nancy & Bob - Exam, about
23 years of age, Nancy, about 18 years of age and Bob, about 2 years of age.
2 March 1819   Peter Simmerman
Teste: Robt W. Greene, S. B. Marshall, James A. Armstrong, William Allen
- April Sessions This bill of sale proved by the oath of Robert W. Greene and
William Allen and ordered registered. [p347/348]

BUCHANAN, John   Bill of Sale   19 May 1819
We, Peter and John Simmerman, of the County of Cumberland and State of
Kentucky have sold to John Buchanan a negro woman named Statia, about
twenty two years of age. 4 March 1819   Peter & John Simmerman
Teste: Alexander Buchanan, Elizabeth Everett, Joshua Armstrong, William
Allen
- April Sessions This bill of sale was proven by the oath of Joshua Armstrong
and William Allen and ordered registered. [p348]

McLEMORE, John C.   Bill of Sale   19 May 1819
We, Peter and John Simmerman of Busksville, Kentucky have sold to John C.
McLemore a certain yellow negro girl by the name of Clarissa, between five and
six years of age. 19 Feb. 1819   Peter & John Simmesman
Teste: John Gunning, Jo Norvell
- April Sessions This bill of sale was proven by the oath of John Gunning and
Joseph Nowell and ordered registered. [p349]

BOSLEY, Beal   Bill of Sale   19 May 1819
I, Green Smithson of the County of Lunenburgh and State of Virginia have sold
to Beal Bosley two negro girls; Jinney, a little inclining to a yellow colour about
fourteen years of age and Beck of a little darker colour about the same age.
22 April 1819   Green Smithson   Wit: Jno. Nichol, James Bell
- April Sessions This bill of sale was acknowledged by Green Smithson and
ordered registered. [349/p350]

FRASER, Donald   Bill of Sale   19 May 1819
I, Pasal Perodeau, have sold to Donald Fraser the following articles of
merchandise: 420 bottles cordial; 168 empty bottles; one handsaw; one ladies
saddle; 6 common candlesticks, 2 brass candlesticks, 2 plated candlesticks, one
stove & pipe, 3 cot beds, 2 bedsteads, 3 feather beds, 12 pair blankets, 12 pair
sheets, 12 pillowcases, 60 liquor kegs and 6 cocks, 4 empty barrels, 1 barrel of
vinegar, 35 gallons gin, one pipe to contain, 1 shew glass, 11 glass jars, 4 one
gallon bottles, 2 pair scales & 2 setts of weights, Sundry confectionary, one brass
Still, one brass pan, one small furnace stove, one pair shovel & tongs, cooking
utensils of every description, one gallon measure, one china press, one Bureau
Desk, on Bureau with drawers, two large dining tables, one dozen silver
teaspoons, one large Silver Dealing Spoon, two Chrystal Decanters and Stands,
two crystal Decanters without stands, fourteen glass tumblers, two setts of china,
two setts of dining ware, one dozen knives & forks, one candle stand, six
window curtains, one dozen of chairs, two looking glasses, 4 tea trays, one gun,
one pair dog irons, one square Marble Rack, one long table.
9 March 1819   Paul Perodeau   Witness: J. Moore
- April Sessions This bill of sale was proven by the oath of J. Moore & ordered
registered. [p350]

CRABB, Henry   Bill of Sale   28 June 1819
I, William Hayes of Warren County, TN, have sold to Henry Crabb one negro
boy, a little past five years old, bright yellow, called in a sale made by Abner
Brown, Merrill, but since called by me and my family, Harry. 10 August 1816
William Hayes   Teste: James Tilford, W. Tannehill
- Nov. Term   This bill of sale was proven by the oath of James Tilford &
Wilkins Tannehill & ordered registered. [p351]

CRABB, Henry   Bill of Sale   28 June 1819
I, John C. Outlaw of Sumner County, TN, together with the undersigned, have
this day sold to Henry Crabb a negro girl named Patsey, aged about fourteen.
5 Aug 1818   Jno. C. Outlaw   Stephen R. Roberts   Edward Charlton
Teste: J. Currey, W. Barrow, M. Barrow
- Nov. Term   This bill of sale was proven by the oaths of J. Currey and W.
Barrow and ordered registered. [pp351/352]

HAYS, Sally   Bill of Sale   16 Aug. 1819
I, Sally Hays, have sold to James Hays a negro man by the name of Ambrose, being eighteen years old. 24 Nov. 1818   Sally (X) Hays
Teste: N. Gooch, James Scott
- July Sessions 1819   This bill of sale proven by the oaths of N. Gooch and James Scott and ordered to be registered. [p352]

DEMOSS, John   Bill of Sale   16 August 1819
I, Sandford Coil of the State of Georgia and County of Burk, have sold to John Demoss a negro man by the name of Harry, between the age of twenty five and thirty years. 16 Feb. 1819   Sanford Coil   Teste: G. B. Taylor, John Hardgrave
- July Sessions   This bill of sale was proven by the oaths of G. B. Taylor and John Hardgrave and ordered to be registered. [pp352/353]

EAST, Edward H.   Deed of Mortgage   16 August 1819
I, David Allen, have sold to Edward H. East one negro woman, aged about nineteen years, named Celia.   27 January 1819   David Allen
Teste: Battersby Balleu, John G. Clements
- It is understood that if the named negro woman die before this mortgage expires, she shall be the loss of Allen and he the said Allen shall be bound to pay the said East his money with interest - And it is also understood that if the said negress lives and Allen redeem said negress the said East may keep the said negress by paying Allen what any two disinterested men shall say the said negress is worth. 27 Jan. 1819   David Allen   Edward H. East
Witness: Battersby Balleau, John G. Clements
- July Sessions   This Deed of Mortgage was proven by the oath of Battersby Balleau and John G. Clements and ordered to be registered. [pp353/354]

CAMPBELL, Patrick W.   Bill of Sale   17 Aug. 1819
I, James Campbell, for the natural love and affection which I bear unto my beloved son Patrick Washington Campbell, give and grand unto the said Patrick W. Campbell the following negroes: one negro woman by the name of Fanny, about twenty three years and her three children, Anthony, Madison & Harriat; also one other girl by the name of Treacy, aged about fifteen years; one negro boy by the name of Joe, aged thirteen years. 21 April 1819
James Campbell Teste: Prestley (X) Shepherd, William P. Campbell
- July Sessions   This bill of sale was acknowledged by the said James Campbell to be his act and deed and ordered to be registered. [p354]

HAYS, James   Bill of Sale   17 August 1819
I, Sally Hays, in consideration of the natural love and affection which I have for my beloved Son, James Hays, also for divers considerations, me the said Sally Hays hereunto moving, have given unto James Hayes a negro woman and child

84

by the names of Edy and Billy; Edy about nineteen and her son, Billy, about two years old. 24 Nov. 1818   Sally (X) Hays   Teste: N. Gooch, James Scott
- July Sessions   This bill of sale proven by the oaths of N. Gooch and James Scott and ordered to be registered. [pp354/355]

LOVELL, James   Bill of Sale   18 August 1819
We, John Barr, William Grimes, Philip Grimes, John Diamond, George R. Lewis, Asa Harriss and Ann Grimes, widow and heirs of William Grimes, Dec'd, do appoint James Lovell our lawful Attorney for the express purpose of exposing to sale a certain negro woman and child, belonging to the estate of William Grimes, Dec'd. Agreeable to advertisement in *The Clarion* paper of 25 August 1818, a woman by the name of Fanny, about 22 years of age, and a boy, her child, by the name of Thomas, aged six years. 22 August 1818   John Barr   William Grimes Philip Grimes John Diamond George R. Lewis Ann Grimes Asa Harriss Valentine A. Gibbs
- I, George P. Allen, one of the Justices of the Peace for the County of Davidson, hereby certify that John Barr, William Grimes, Philip Grimes by his Agent, George P. Lewis, John Diamond, George R. Lewis, Asa Harriss and Ann Grimes appeared this day before me and acknowledged the foregoing Power of Attorney to James Lovell. 22 August 1818   G. S. Allen, J. P.   [pp355/356]

HEATON, Thomas   Bill of Sale   18 August 1819
I have sold to Thomas Heaton a certain negro man named Joshua. 16 July 1819   C. Stump   Teste: Rich'd H. Barry, R. Weakley
- July Sessions This bill of sale was acknowledged by Christopher Stump as his act and ordered to be registered. [p356]

HEATON, Thomas   Bill of Sale   18 August 1819
We, Stump and Daniel have sold unto Thomas Heaton a negro man, Austin, about forty years of age. 16 July 1819   Stump & Daniel
Teste: J. J. Henton, R. Weakley
- July Sessions This bill of sale was acknowledged by C. Stump to be his act and ordered to be registered. [p357]

GRIMES, Willam [heirs]   Article of Agreement   18 August 1819
Article of Agreement made this 12 September 1818 between Ann Grimes of the one part and John Barr, William Grimes, Philip Grimes, George R. Lewis, John Diamond, Valentine A. Gibbs and Asa Harris of the other: whereas Ann Grimes was left 160 acres of land and a negro woman and child, woman by the name of Fanny and child, a boy named Thomas, for her natural life or widowhood, by the last Will of William Grimes, Deceased. It has now been agreed that the land and negroes shall be sold and that she will take a childs part of said sale, to wit one ninth part of the amount of the sale of said negroes and land.

George R. Lewis   Ann (X) Grimes   Jno. Diamond   John (X) Barr   Asa
Harriss   Valentine A. Gibbs   William (X) Grimes   Philip Grimes
At-est: Jams Lovell, John (X) Bell
  - January Sessions 1819   This Article of Agreement between Ann Grimes, John
Barr, William Grimes, Philip Grimes, George R. Lewis, John Diamond, Asa
Harris and Valentine A. Gibbs was proven to be the act of the said John, Wm,
Philip, George R., John, Asa and Valentine by the oath of James Lovell and
ordered to be registered. [pp357/358]

CRABB, Henry   Bill of Sale   18 August 1819
I, Willie Barrow, in consideration of a negro girl, Patsy, and two hundred dollars
in cash, have sold to Henry Crabb a negro man of a black colour, aged about
thirty years, named Moses. 27 May 1819   W. Barrow
Wts: John Stephens, David Barrow
  - July Sessions   This bill of sale proven by the oath of John Stephens and David
Barrow and ordered to be registered. [p358]

READ, Jones   Bill of Sale   18 August 1819
I, Thomas J. Read, have sold to Jonas Read the following negro slaves: Viney,
a woman about 26 years of age; Bob, her Son about four years of age; Mineva,
her daughter about three years of age; Harrison, her son about nine months old;
Charity a woman about fifteen/sixteen years of age and her child. 15 Jan. 1819
      Th. J. Read   Witness: Jno Price, Jos. Jno Sumner
  - July Sessions   This Bill of Sale was acknowledged by the said Thomas J. to be
his act and deed and ordered registered. [pp358/359]

READ, John A.   Deed of Gift   18 August 1819
I, Jones Read, for the consideration of the love and affection I have for my
grandson John A. Read, Son of Thomas J. Read, give him, the said John Read,
two negroes, a boy the the name of Bill and a girl by the name of Leviney. 20
July 1819   Jones Read
  - July Sessions   A Deed of Gift was acknowledged by the said Jones Read and
ordered to be registered. [p359]

TURNER, James H.   Deed of Gift
                18 August 1819
I, Jones Read, for the love and affection I have for my Grandson James H.
Turner give him two negroes, a boy by the name of John, now in my possession,
and a girl by the name of Melinda, in the possession of John Frazer. I warrant
the title unto the said James H. Turner & his heirs forever, that is if the said
James should have any heirs by his lawful wife, otherwise should the said James
F Turner depart this life without any such heirs then the two negroes, John &
Melinda, shall return to my sons and daughters.   19 Apr 1819   Jones Read

- Deed of Gift was acknowledged by the said Jones Read to be his act and ordered registered. [p359/360]

HYDE, Tazewell   Bill of Sale   20 August 1819
I have this day sold to Tazewell Hyde the following property: 8 Beds, Furniture & Bedsteads; 1 Side Board; 1 Piano Forte; 1 Desk; 1 Bureau; 1 Set Dining Tables; 1 Dining Table; 4 Small Tables; 1 pr Look Glasses; 1 pr Brass & Iron fire fender, shovel & tongs; 2 pr candle shades; 1 candle stand; 1 sugar chest; 2 doz. Windsor chairs; 3 small Windsor chairs; 12 common chairs; 1 chest drawers; 1 bookcase; 2 sets flower pots; 3 trunks; 4 maps, 1 pr small andirons; 3 doz. china plates, 6 china dishes; 4 china pitchers, 5 Teaboards, 1 1/2 doz common plates; 6 dishes; 2 tureens, 3 dozen knives & forks; 6 dozen glass tumblers, 1 pair salt cellars; 3 sugar dishes; 4 Decanters, 2 Brass kettles, 3 large pots, 5 kettles, 2 skillets, 1 pair brass candlesticks, 1 tea chest, 1 pair candle snuffers & tray; 2 side saddles and 2 bridles, 2 churns, 6 pails, 1 set carpeting for large room, 1 set carpeting for small room, 3 tea pots, 1 set castors, 1/2 dozen silver table spoons, 1 soup spoon, 1 dozen silver spoons, 1 cupboard, 1 carriage & gears, 2 pair glass candle shades. All of which property delivery is made to said Tazewell but the same is not carried away by him from the residence of the said John Stump but is left there in loan to the sister of said Tazewell who is the wife of said John and the said Tazewell is to have free privilege to take possession thereof whenever he shall see proper 19 July 1819
    Jno. Stump   Witness: Tho King, Sam King
- July Sessions This bill of sale was acknowledged by the said John Stump and ordered to be registered. [p361]

WOOD, Fleming C.   Power of Attorney   9 Sept. 1819
I, Peter Little of the City of Natchez in the State of Mississippi, have appointed Fleming C. Wood my true & lawful attorney and in my name to sell a certain negro man now confined in the Nashville Jail, named Simon, about twenty six years old. 9 Aug. 1819   Peter Little
- Be it known that on the day of the date here of before me, John Henderson, Notary Public for the State of Mississippi, residing in the City of Natchez, by lawful authority duly commissioned and sworn, came Peter Little and acknowledged the foregoing Power of Attorney. 10 Aug 1819   John Henderson Notr. Pub. [pp361/362]

SHELBY, John   Bill of Sale   9 Sept. 1819
I, Peter Randolph, sell to John Shelby a certain negro man named John, of the age of thirty three years. 19 Jan. 1819   Peter Randolph
- January Sessions This bill of sale was acknowledged by Peter Randolph to be his Act & Deed and ordered to be registered. [p362]

SNOW, David C.   Bill of Sale   9 Sept. 1819
I, William H. Hamblen, have sold to David C. Snow a negro girl named
Charlotte, of the age of fifteen years. 29 Sept 1818   W. H. Hamblen
Witness: Jacob Williams
- July Sessions   This bill of sale was acknowledged by William H. Hamblen
and ordered to be registered. [pp362/363]

SHUTE, John   Bill of Sale   6 October 1819
I, Thomas Shute obligate myself to John Shute for the purpose of securing him
for being security in obtaining an injunction against John McNairy and Robert
Weakley in a Suit now in a Court of Equity in Nashville and for the purpose
above mentioned sell unto him two negro boys being my negro woman Lydia's
two oldest boys and named Reuben & Henry. 19 April 1819   Thomas Shute
Teste: Lee Shute, H. F. Nowell
- July Sessions   This bill of sale was proven by the oaths of Lee Shute and H.
F. Newell and ordered to be registered. [p363]

SHUTE, John   Bill of Sale   6 October 1819
I, Christopher Stump, have sold to John Shute a negro man by the name of
Daniel, about thirty years of age. 12 June 1819 C. Stump Teste: Philip Shute
- July Sessions   This bill of sale was acknowledged by said Christopher Stump
and ordered to be registered. [pp363/364]

PRYOR, Nicholas B.   Bill of Sale   13 October 1819
I have sold to Nicholas B. Pryor a negro man slave by the name of Jim, a
carpenter. The said Jim having been purchased jointly by said Pryor and
myself, it is intended to sell my half only 11 June 1819   Sam Elam
Teste: Washington Perkins, Martin Clark
- July Sessions   This bill of sale was acknowledged by the said Elam and
ordered to be registered. [p364]

WASHINGTON, Gilbert G.   Deed of Trust   14 October 1819
Samuel Elan in order to secure the following debt due by note in the Branch
Bank, which said debt was executed by Elam and endorsed by Gilbert G.
Washington and William Carroll ... said Elam does deliver to Gilbert G.
Washington a certain negro woman named Anna. Gilbert G. Washington shall
as soon as convenient shall advertise and sell said negro woman and pay and
satisfy all charges and the residue of the monies if any to be paid to the said
Samuel Elan. 11 May 1819   Sam. Elam Teste: Joseph Keen, Jos. D. Murray
- July Sessions   This Deed of Trust was acknowledged by Elam and ordered
registered. [pp364/365]

VAUGHN, David   Deed of Trust   14 October 1819
Willie Barrow sells to David Vaughn four negro men slaves; Sam, Nero, Willoughby and John, between the ages of twenty and thirty years. In Trust - Willie purchased of George M. Deadrick in his lifetime part of Lot #24 in the Town of Nashville and house - it being the house and part of Lot whereon Anthony Johnson and Richmond and Flint at present reside; Willie has sold the said part of said lot to Michael C. Dunn, Thomas Edmiston, John Bowles, Samuel Crockett and David Vaughn ... slaves are to secure debt.
20 July 1819   W. Barrow   Teste: O. B. Hayes, Robt H. Adams
- July Sessions This Deed of Trust was proved by the oaths of O. B. Hayes and Robt H. Adams and ordered registered. [pp365/366]

DREWRY, John   Bill of Sale   11 Nov. 1819
I, John Criddle, Sen'r, have sold to John Drewry a negro woman slave named Sally for notes on *Stump and Cox*. I do not warrant her to be sound and healthy as she has had the white swelling on one arm and one leg. 23 October 1819   Jno. Criddle   Witness: Wm Adams
- October Sessions This bill of sale was acknowledged by John Criddle and ordered to be registered. [p367]

DREWRY, John   Bill of Sale   11 Nov. 1819
I, John Criddle, have sold to John Drewry two negro girls named Prudance and Biddy, aged about four and two years old. 30 Oct. 1819   Jno. Criddle
Witness:
- October Sessions This bill of sale was acknowledged by John Criddle and ordered registered. [p367]

EAST, Edward H.   Bill of Sale   11 Nov. 1819
I, Isaac L. Crow, have sold to Edward H. East one negro woman named Ceila.
16 June 1819   Teste: James Carter, Joseph Vaulx
- October Sessions This bill of Sale was proven by the oath of James Carter & Joseph Vaulx and ordered registered. [p368]

LESTER, John   Bill of Sale   11 Nov. 1819
I, John Lester, have sold to Richard Lester one negro girl named Silvey, aged eight years. 3 Aug 1819 John Lester
Teste: Wm Moss, D. P. Davis, Alexander Lester
- October Sessions This bill of sale was proven by the oath of D. P. Davis and ordered to be certified. [p368]

McLENDON, Dennis   Bill of Sale   11 Nov. 1819
We have sold to Dennis McLendon a negro girl slave named Patty, about twelve years of age. 15 Sept. 1819   G. W. Banton, Lewis Banton

Teste: William Huggins, John Huggins
- October Sessions This bill of sale was proven by the oath of William Huggins and John Huggins and ordered registered. [pp368/369]

NICHOLS, John   Bill of Sale   11 Nov. 1819
I, Alfred Nichols have this day sold to John Nichols of Williamson County a negro man by the name of Jacob, about the age of twenty five years - paid to James McGavock for Adam; paid to Hewlett & Harper & jail fees; paid Cox for two execution, Snow and Johnston; said John went security for me to William Reed. 20 April 1819   A. Nichols   Witness: T. Weston
- October Sessions This bill of sale was proven by the oath of Thomas Weston and ordered certified. [p369]

READ, Jones   Bill of Sale   11 Nov. 1819
I, Thomas J. Read, have sold to Jones Read the following articles of household and kitchen furniture: Books, 3 feather bed Bolsters and pillows, 2 hair mattresses, 4 bedsteads, two bureaus, 1 looking glass, 2 dressing glasses, 3 tables, 1 work stand, 1 kitchen cupboard, 1 sugarchest, 1 set blue dining ware, 1 set teaware, 6 large silver spoons, 12 silver teaspoons, 2 doz. knives & forks, 12 glass tumblers, 1 set plated castors, 5 flower potts, 2 pair of brass andirons, 2 pair shovel & tongs, 2 floor carpets, 1 hearth rug, 1 passage carpet, 1 secretarys desk, 13 windsor chairs, 15 pair blankets, 12 pair cotton & linen sheets, 7 bed covers, 1 Red Morocco workbox, 3 tubs, 6 pails, 2 large waiters, 1 saddle & bridle; the following books - 1 vol. life of Mrs. Cooper, 1 vol. *Buchanon's Philosophy*, 1 vol. *Historical Register, Haywoods Reports, Portrature of Methodism*, 6 vols. *Fletchers Checks*, 1 vol. Wesley on *Original Sin*, 1 vol. *Psalms & Hymns*, 1 vol. *Johnstons Dictionary*, 1 vol. *Christian Morals*, 1 Family Bible, 1 vol. *Bucks Dictionary*, 1 vol. Methodist Magazine, one hymn book, 4 vols. *Farmers Observations*, Hlopstocks Mesiah, *Life of Doctor Coke*, Woods *Dictionary of the Bible*, 2 vols *Meckles Travels*, 1 vol. Fletchers *Appeal and Life*, 1 vol. Herveys *Meditations*, 1 vol. New Testament, 1 vol. 1 print of Washington, 6 prints Naval Officers, 2 kettles, 3 potts, 2 ovens and a bay filley, two years old last spring, which is not at Jones Reads.
22 Oct. 1819   Th. J. Read   Witness: Tho. H. Fletcher
- October Sessions This bill of sale was acknowledged by Thomas J. Read and ordered registered. [pp369/370]

CROW, Isaac L.   Bill of Sale   12 Nov. 1819
Whereas at April Sessions 1819 Isaac L. Crow recovered a judgment against David Allan and George W. Charlton and writ was issued; writ came to the hands of Thomas Hickman esquire, Sheriff, who levied the same on a negro woman named Celia, as the property of David Allen; after due notice said

woman was sold to Isaac L. Crow this 27 Oct. 1819. Tho. Hickman, Shff
Teste: Nathan Ewing, Henry Ewing
- October Sessions This bill of sale was acknowledged by Tho. Hickman and ordered recorded.
[pp 370/371]

STUMP, Albert G.   Bill of Sale   12 Nov. 1819
I, Richard Hyde, have this day sold to Albert Gallston Stump, son of John Stump, a negro man named Isom, aged twenty years. 26 Feb. 1813 Richard Hyde Teste: Tazewell Hyde, Jourdan Hyde
- October Sessions This bill of sale was proved by the oath of Taswell Hyde and Jourdan Hyde and ordered registered. [p371]

SHUTE, Philip   Bill of Sale   12 Nov. 1819
I, Christopher Stump, have sold to Philip Shute six negroes: David, about thirty five years of age; Alsey, a woman about nineteen and her child about two months old; Patsey, about ten years of age; Joe, about six years of age; Fanny, about four years of age. 28 Sept. 1819 C. Stump Teste: Rich'd H. Barry, Jno. J. Hinton
- October Sessions This bill of sale was proved by the oath of Richard H. Barry and John J. Hinton and ordered registered. [pp371/372]

SHUTE, Thomas   Bill of Sale   12 Nov. 1819
I, Christopher Stump, have sold to Thomas Shute all my household furniture as follows: one pair of Glasses Chimney ornaments, 1 sideboard, mantle glass, one set tables, 4 beds & furniture, glass belonging to sideboard, one dressing glass, dining *chaney*, breakfast *chaney*, all the carpeting belonging to the house, 2 doz. chairs, 1 desk, 4 pair of hand irons and many other things of little value.
3 Oct. 1819 C. Stump Teste: Rich'd H. Barry, John J. Hinton
- This bill of sale was proven by the oath of Richard H. Barry and John J. Hinton and ordered registered. [p373]

VAUGHN, David   Bill of Sale   15 Nov. 1819
I, R. A. Higginbotham, have sold to David Vaughn all the goods, household stuff, implements and furniture: 1 breakfast table, 1 dining table, 2 dozen windsor chairs, 1 sugar chest, 1 candle stand, 1 work table, 2 dressing tables, 1 secretary & bookcase, 1 small chase, 4 beds & furniture, 4 brass candle sticks, 2 pair plated candle sticks, 1/2 doz Tablespoons, silver, 1/2 doz Desert Silver Spoons, 1 doz teaspoons, silver, 1 sideboard, 4 doz. plates, 1 bureau, 1 cradle, 1 fire fender, 1 set fire dogs & shovel & tongs, 2 carpets, 2 rugs, 1/2 doz dishes, 3 teapots, 2 coffee pots, 3 bottles, 6 pitchers, 1 silver watch, 1 gold watch, Ladies, one horse saddle & bridle, one bay mare, bridle & side saddle.
7 Sept 1819 R. A. Higgenbotham Teste: J. H. Green, Joseph Gould
- October Sessions This bill of sale was acknowledged by the said Reuben A.

Higginbotham and ordered registered. [pp372/373]

POTTS, Hamilton A.   Bill of Sale   16 Nov. 1819
I have this day sold to Hamilton A. Potts a negro named Jim, about sixteen years
of age. 21 June 1819 John Catron   Teste: Andrew Hayes, Thomas Washington
- This bill of sale was acknowledged by John Catron and ordered registered.
[p373]

POTTS, Ann Mariah   Bill of Sale   16 Nov. 1819
I, John Criddle, sell to Mrs. Ann Meriah Potts one negro woman, known by the
name of Kittey. 17 June 1819 John Criddle   Teste: Robert Lanier, John Catron
- July Sessions   This bill of sale was proved by the oath of Jno. Catron and
ordered registered. [p374]

WATSON, William W.   Bill of Sale   29 Nov. 1819
I, Benjamin Atkinson, have sold to William Watson the following household
furniture: 3 feather beds, 6 sheets, 6 blankets, 3 quilts, 1 pair brass andirons, 1
pair shovel & tongs, one gilt frame looking glass, 2 half worn carpets, 1/2 doz.
large silver table spoons, 1 soup ladle, 1 doz. silver teaspoons, 1/2 pint silver
tumbler. 29 Sept. 1819   Benj. Atkingson   Teste: Wm Garner, John Sowers
- Nov. Term   This bill of sale was acknowledged by Benjamin Atkinson and
ordered registered. [pp374/375]

CANTRELL, Stephen   Bill of Sale   22 Dec. 1819
Ota Cantrell, of the county of Rutherford and State of Tennessee, in return to
money credited in favor of Ota Cantrell upon an account existing against said
Ota Cantrell in favour of said Stephen Cantrell & Co. does sell to Stephen
Cantrell, Jr. & Co. a wagon and five horses together with the harness and chains
belonging to said wagon and five horses. [4 bay horses and 1 mouse coloured
horse] Ota Cantrell is to have the use and possession of said wagon and horses
for the term of six months. 1 Dec. 1819 Ota Cantrell   Teste: Robt. H. Adams
- Nov. Term   This bill of sale was acknowledged by Ota Cantrell and ordered
registered. [p375]

CATRON, John   Bill of Sale   18 Jan. 1820
John Catron recovered two judgments before John Stump Esquire, a Justice of
the Peace, against James Potts, which executions thereon William M. Hinton, as
Constable, levied the judgements upon a negro woman, named Kitty, as the
property of James Potts. Said negro woman was sold to satisfy the executions
and John Catron became the highest and best bidder. 27 Dec. 1819
W. M. Hinton [see probate at the end of next] [p376]

POTTS, Ann Moriah & Eliza   Bill of Sale   18 Jan. 1820
John Catron, being the same named in the above bill of sale, doth hereby sell unto Ann Maria Potts a negro woman named Kitty, being the same slave above mention in the bill of sale from William M. Hinton to John Catron. Subject in part to the following trust; said Ann Maria Potts shall hold the one half of the interest in said negro woman Kitty and her increase for the use and benefit of her sister Eliza Potts and be compelled to make a legal title toward Eliza at any time the latter may require it. 3 Jan. 1820   John Catron
- Nov. Term The foregoing two bills of sale from William M. Hinton to John Catron and from John Catron to Ann Maria Potts & Eliza Potts for a negro woman named Kitty was acknowledged by William M. Hinton and John Catron and ordered registered. 5 Jan. 1820

BARROW, Matthew   Bill of Sale   21 Feb. 1820
I, Meredith Jordon, have sold to Matthew Barrow a negro man slave named Nat, aged about twenty one. 17 Jan. 1820   Meredith (X) Jourdon
Witness: Ephraim H. Foster, Boyd McNairy
- January Sessions This bill of sale proven by the oath of Ephriam H. Foster & Boyd McNairy and ordered registered. [p377]

CAMPBELL, William P.   Bill of Sale   21 Feb. 1820
We have sold to William P. Campbell a negro boy about fourteen years of age, named Sam. 7 Sept 1819   G. W. Banton Lewis Banton
Teste: P. W. Campbell, John B. Seat
- January Sessions This bill of sale was proven by the oath of P. W. Campbell and John B. Seat and ordered registered. [pp377/378]

CRIDDLE, John Senr   Bill of Sale   21 Feb. 1820
I have sold to John Criddle, Senr the following blacksmiths tools: two anvils, two pair bellows, 2 blacksmith vices, 2 screw plates, 1 sledge hammer, 3 hand hammers, 8 pair blacksmith tongs, 1 set of blacksmith shoeing tools.
29 Dec. 1819   Stp'n Sutton   Witness: Jno. S. Cox, Robert Lanier
- January Sessions This bill of sale Stephen Sutton to John Criddle was proven by the oath of John S. Cox and Robert Lanier. [p378]

SOMMERVILLE & CRUTCHER   Deed of Trust   21 Feb. 1820
Alpha Kingsley for the sum of six dollars, have sold to John Sommerville and Thomas Crutcher the following articles of personal property: one negro woman named Jenny, girl Harriet and boy Isam, 2 horses, 4 cows with calves, 2 sows & pigs, 1 secretary and bookcase, library containing 200 books, 3 large looking glasses, 1 mahogany frame sofa, 40 windsor chairs, 1 set dining tables, 1 breakfast table, 1 settee, 1 sideboard, 1 ladies workstand, 2 caskets, one china press, one sugar chest, 3 bureaus, 4 toilet tables, 4 glasses, ten beds, bedsteads

& bed furniture, 10 diaper tablecloths, 2 damask tablecloths, 5 doz. knives & forks, 3 carving knives & forks, 2 sets dining china, one of Canton and one of Liverpool, 2 sets tea china, one of French, one of English, Liverpool coffee cups & saucers, Silverplate, one tea and one water pot, one sugar, one creamer and one slop bowl, 2 doz. tablespoons, 2 1/2 doz teaspoons, 7 best tea decanters, 2 doz. wine glasses, 2 doz. tumblers, 6 goblets, 4 gallon bottles, 24 quart bottles, 6 glass jars, 4 stone jars, 4 china pitchers, 4 wash stands, 6 wash basins, 1 gold watch, 3 pr brass andirons, two brass fenders and 2 shovels & tongs, 4 teaboards, 6 waiters, 6 brass and 2 plated candlesticks, 4 steel and 2 plated snuffers and snuffer trays, 2 demijons. kitchen furniture; 1 large kettle, 2 large pots, 2 dinner pots, 3 bake or dutch ovens, one biscuit oven, 2 tea kettles, coffee boiler, 2 coffee pots, coffee mill, 3 tables, 1 safe, spider frying pan, one griddle, 4 water piggins, 2 milk piggins, 2 stone pans, 4 tin pans. In Trust to secure debt to the Branch Bank of the State of Tennessee at Nashville. 17 Aug. 1819
        Alpha Kingsley   Witness: John Spence, Cha. C. Trabue
- January Sessions   This Deed of Trust was proven by the oath of John Spence and Charles C. Trabue and ordered registered. [pp378/379/380]

SOMMERVILLE & CRUTCHER   Deed of Trust   21 Feb. 1820
Alpha Kingsley, for six dollars and other considerations him thereunto moving, conveys to John Sommerville and Thomas Cruther the following articles of personal property: 2 saddles & bridles, 2 hand bellows, 2 sets mantle ornaments, 3 family portraits, 1 barrel whiskey, 1 barrels vinegar, 4 shovel & tongs, 4 andirons, 3 floor carpets, 1 passage & 2 stair carpets, 1 table castors, 4 china pitchers, 2 doz. tumblers, 2 knife boxes, 1 brass kettle, 2 bellmettle kettles, 7 dishcovers, 1 woodsaw, 1 barrel flour, 4 servant beds & bedding, 1 barrel cog. brandy, 1/4 cast Tenneriffe wine, 1/4 cast Madeira wine, 1/2 cast Port, 1 barrel coffee, 1 barrel brown sugar, 100 lbs loaf sugar, 6,000 lbs bacon, 400 lbs salted & smoked beef, 50 lbs candles, 20 cord wood, 20 barrels corn and one ton hay. In Trust to secure payment of debt to the Branch Bank of the State of Tennessee at Nashville. 1 Sept 1820   Alpha Kingsley
Teste: Chas C. Trabue, Ephraim H. Foster
- January Sessions   This Deed of Trust was acknowledged by the said Kingsley and ordered to be registered. [pp381/382]

BARRY, Richard H.   Bill of Sale   22 Feb. 1820
I, Christopher Stump, have sold to Richard H. Barry all my claim and interest in a negro man by the name of Pulaski, a stonemason, it being the interest of James T. Barry, William L. Barry and John G. Barry, heirs of William T. Barry, deceased, and from them being conveyed to me. 19 Oct. 1819 C. Stump
Teste: Philip Shute, Jno J. Hinton
- October Sessions   This bill of Sale was proven by the oath of Philip Shute and John J. Hinton and ordered registered. [pp382/383]

WOOD, Alexander H.   Bill of Sale   22 Feb. 1820
I, William Crockett of the County of Sumner and State of Tennessee, have sold
to Alexander H. Wood a certain female coloured slave called Patsey, between
the age of sixteen and seventeen years. 27 Jan. 1820   William Crockett
Teste: P. H. Martin
- January Sessions This bill of sale was acknowledged by William Crockett to
be his act and ordered to be registered. [p383]

FAIRFAX, Cecelia   Bill of Sale   22 Feb. 1820
Received from Cecelia Fairfax the value from the following articles sold to
satisfy an execution which John Howlett obtained against Nathaniel Peck and
one execution which W. Pulliam obtained against said Peck. One negro woman
named Amy, about forty years old, lame in one arm; one bureau, 6 chairs, 1
cupboard & furniture, 1 candlestand, 1 table, 1 bed & furniture, 1 dressing glass,
one looking glass, 17 boxes, 1 grindstone, 4 potts, ovens, 1 lot cooperware, 1 set
smoothing irons. William Howlett, Constable
- January Sessions This bill of sale was acknowledged by William Howlett as
constable and ordered to be registered. [383/384]

FOSTER, Ephraim H.   Deed of Trust   22 Feb. 1820
I, Thomas Eastland, have sold to Ephraim H. Foster the following personal
property & household furniture: 5 featherbeds, 3 mattresses, 4 low post poplar
bedsteads, 1 high cherry bed, 1 high bureau, 16 pair of linen & cotton sheets, 16
pair pillowcases, 8 pair rose blankets, 4 pair plain blankets, 6 white
counterpanes, 4 checked counterpanes, 2 chintz counterpanes, 1 set chintz bed
curtains, 1 set chintz window curtains, 1 mahogany bureau & glass, 1 large quilt,
framed looking glass, 1 pair card tables, 2 small dressing tables, 1 cherry dining
table, 1 pair large brass andirons, 1 hearth fender, 2 pr brass /headed shovel &
tongs, 2 pr cut glass decanters, 1 case bottles, 4 dozen Liverpool breakfast and
dining plates, 1 doz. Liverpool dishes, 1 set blue china teacups and saucers, 1
dozen blue coffee cups and saucers, one blue wash bowl & pitcher, two dozen
white ivory handled dinner knives & forks, 2 dozen ivory handled breakfast
knives & forks, 1 doz silver tablespoons, 1 doz. teaspoons, 2 dutch ovens, 1
large kettle and 3 pots, one teakettle, one coffee mill, one London Mahogany
Pianoforte, one walnut desk & bookcase, one floor carpet, one hearth rug, one
pair plated candlesticks, one pair plated snuffer & tray, two pair brass
candlesticks, two teaboards, one dozen red windsor chairs, gilt back, one
counting room desk. In Trust - I am indebted to Russell Williams.
21 Jan. 1820   Thos. Eastland
- January Sessions This Deed of Trust was acknowledged by Thomas Eastland
and ordered to be registered. [pp384/385]

GRIZZARD, Edmund   Deed of Mortgage   22 Feb. 1820
Thomas Moorefield has sold the following furniture to Edmund Grizzard: one
high post bedstead & sacking bottom with one stand curtains, one featherbed,
one pair blankets, 1 pair sheets, one counterpain, one secretary, one sugar chest,
one breakfast table, one dining table, one dressing table, six chairs, four trunks,
one teaboard, five wine glasses, four tumblers, one decanter, two set knives &
forks, two sets plated, one set teaware, one pitcher, one shovel & tongs, one pair
andirons, one brass kettle, one tea kettle, two ovens, three skillets, one pot, one
iron kettle, one tin pans, two tin buckets, two pans, two piggins, six stone jars,
one cow & calf, one dressing glass and two band boxes.
€ Dec. 1819   Thos. Moorefield   Teste: John S. Topp, M. Fly
- January Sessions This Deed of Mortgage was acknowledged by Thomas
Moorefield and ordered to be registered. [pp386/387]

GLEAVES, Michael   Bill of Sale   22 Feb. 1820
We, William Caldwell, Sr. and William Caldwell, Jr, have sold to Michael
Gleaves a negro woman and children, whose names and ages are as follows:
Priscilla, aged 20 years, Ransom, the eldest child, a son aged 4 years, Emily, the
second child, a girl aged 2 years, Lidia, the third child, aged 7 months.
15 Jan. 1820   Wm Caldwell, Sr.   Wm Caldwell, Jr.
Teste: A. Ritchey, David B. Love
- January Sessions This bill of sale was acknowledged by William Caldwell,
Senr and Junr and ordered to be registered. [p387]

GOODWIN, William W. & wife   Deed of Gift   23 February 1820
I, Bennett Blackman for the love and affection I have unto my daughter Anney
Blackman, now Anny Goodwin, and my son in law William W. Goodwin, and
also for the better maintenance, support and lively hood of them have granted
unto the said Anny and W. W. Goodwin, their heirs and assigns forever the
following negroes and property: one negro woman named Betty, one negro girl
named Viney, one negro boy named Hardy; children of the woman Betty, one
horse, bridle & saddle, two cows and calves, one bed, bedstead and furniture.
23 January 1818   B. Blackman   Teste: Nicholas Tomlin, John Blackman
- January Sessions This deed of gift, Bennett Blackman to William W. Goodwin
and Ann his wife, was proven by the oath of Nicholas Tomlin and John
Blackman and ordered to be registered. [pp387/388]

JOYCE, Thomas   Deed of Gift   23 February 1820
I, Bennett Blackman for the love and affection I have unto my daughter Charlotte
Blackman, now C. Joice, and my son in law Thomas Joice, and also for the
better maintenance, support and livelihood of them, have given unto the said C.
and T. Joice the following negroes and property; one negro woman named Clara
and one negro girl named Morgan, [given in the year 1814 and their increase

from that time] and one negro named Bryant; one horse, bridle & saddle; two cows and calves; one bed, bedstead & furniture. 23 January 1818

Bennett Blackman   Teste: Nicholas Tomlin, John Blackman
- January Sessions This deed of gift, Bennett Blackman to Thomas Joyce and Charlotte, his wife, was proven by the oath of Nicholas Tomlin and John Blackman and ordered to be registered. [pp388/389]

McCASLIN, William   Bill of Sale   23 February 1820
I, Austin M. Coats, have sold to William McCaslin a negro boy named Hubbard, aged eleven. 2 Dec. 1819   Austin M. Coats
Teste: John Pirtle, Abemilech Herring
- January Sessions This bill of sale was proven by the oath of John Pirtle and Abemileck Herrin and ordered to be registered. [pp389/390]

MOLLOY/TRIM, sOPHIA   Bill of Sale   23 February 1820
I, John Deatherage, have received of Sophia Molloy alias Sophia Trim, wife of Trim the Barber, one hundred dollars in full for a negro girl named Myra, about four years of age and do obligate and bind myself to emancipate and set free the said negro girl Myra at the ensuing County Court of Davidson and do also agree to make a condition in the said emancipation that the said girl shall be bound to serve said Sophia until she arrives at the age of twenty two years and to her heirs and assigns. This contract is with said Sophia individually and independent of her husband, Trim, and the said Sophia is to have all the benefit of the services of Myra until she arrives at the age of twenty two years free and unrestrained from the control of her said husband, Trim. 3 December 1814   John Deatherage
  Witness: Robert Searcy, Jno C. McLemore
- January Sessions This bill of sale was proven by the oath of John C. McLemore and ordered to be registered. [p390]

SUMNER, Duke W.   Bill of Sale   23 February 1820
I, Eli Talbot, have sold to Duke W. Sumner a certain negro man slave named Lee. 1 July 1819 Eli Talbot
- This bill of sale was acknowledged by Eli Talbot to be his act and deed and ordered to be registered. [pp390/391]

SAUNDERS, Francis   Bill of Sale   23 February 1820
I have sold to Francis Saunders a negro girl named Katy. 6 Nov. 1819
Philip Shiveley   Teste: James (X) Pigg, Pierce P. Pigg
- January Sessions This bill of sale was proven by the oath of James Pigg and Pierce P. Pigg and ordered to be registered. [p391]

SAUNDERS, Francis   Bill of Sale   23 February 1820
I have sold to Francis Saunders a negro woman named Thursday and her child

named Helener. 6 Nov. 1819   Philip Shiveley
Witness: James (X) Pigg, Pierce P. Pigg
- January Sessions This bill of sale was proven by the oath of James Pigg and
Pierce P. Pigg and ordered to be registered. [p391]

ROPER, Robert and William, Jr.   Bill of Sale   23 February 1820
I, Andrew Gilkerson of Montgomery County and State of Pennsylvania, have
sold to Robert and William Roper, Jr. a negro girl named Anne, about ten years
of age. Andrew Gilkerson 19 May 1812 Teste: B. S. Bradford, Joseph Korp
- April Sessions 1813 This bill of sale was proven by the oath of Benjamin J.
Bradford and Joseph Korp [p392]

SEAL, William   Bill of Sale   23 February 1820
*[there is a notation to see page 284] {original page #}
I, James W. Glasgow, having arrived at lawful age do now validate and make
good the within signature, it having been executed when I was a minor.
2 Dec. 1819 Jas W. Glasgow   Teste: W. P. Campbell, Will P. Owen
- January Sessions a confirmation of a bill of sale, James W. Glasgow and
James Glasgow to William P. Seat, was proven by the oath of William P.
Campbell and William P. Owen and ordered to be registered. [p392]

WEAKLEY, Robert   Bill of Sale   23 February 1820
I, Archibald H. Harris of the town of Jefferson in Rutherford County and State
of Tennessee, have this day sold to Robert Weakley a negro man slave by the
name of Herculas, about twenty one years old. ... do further promise to have the
transfer of a bill of sale made by David Shelby of Sumner County and State of
Tennessee on 25 December last, for said Hercules to me put on record in the
county of Sumner, the better to secure title to said negro to Robert Weakley.
Jan. 2, 1819 A. H. Harris   Teste: Jas. H. Weakley, Robert L. Weakley
- January Sessions This bill of sale was proven by the oath of James H.
Weakley and ordered to be registered. [p393]

WEAKLEY, Robert   Bill of Sale   23 February 1820
I, William McGee of Person County and State of North Carolina, have sold to
Robert Weakley two negro boys, one by the name of Aaron about seven years
old, and Lewis, about fourteen years old...further bind myself that said negroes
are sound and healthy except the scald head of Lewis. January 6, 1819
    William McGee   Teste: C. Stump, J. W. Clay
- January Sessions This bill of sale was proven by the oath of C. Stump and
ordered to be certified. [p394]

McNAIRY, John   Bill of Sale   24 February 1820
I, Thomas H. Fletcher, have sold to John McNairy a negro woman named Polly,

aged 35 years; a negro woman named Fanny, aged 18 years; and a negro girl named Rhoda, aged 12 years. Sept 14, 1819 Tho H. Fletcher
Teste: J. Gordon
 - January Sessions This bill of sale was proven by the oath of James Gordon and ordered to be registered. [p394]

DICKINSON, William Thos, Guardn Deed of Relinquishment 10 March 1820
By a bill of sale bearing date 22 December 1817, I purchased of William Thomas Dickinson nine negro slaves: Bob, about twenty one years old; Mitchell, about nineteen years old; Cate, about forty five; Flora, about seventeen; Aggy, about sixteen; Mary, about ten; Cloe, about eight; Ben, about four; and Peter, about one year old and whereas on the 25th of October 1819 I returned said negroes and also Delila, the child of Cate, to Mr. Francis McKay, guardian for said William Thomas, in return of by bill of sale ... I now reconvey to said Francis and quitclaim to the same negroes and also to the child Delia above said the daughter of Cate and also to Margaret, daughter of Agga, born since the redelivery. 17 January 1820 Joseph Philips
 - January Sessions   This deed of relinquishment, Joseph Philips to Francis McKay, Guardian for William Thomas Dickinson, was acknowledged by Joseph Philips and ordered registered. [p395]

LESTER, Alexander   Bill of Sale   10 March 1820
I, John Lester, sell a negro girl by the name of Phillis to Alexander Lester. 17 May 1819 John Lester, Senr   Teste: Jesse Smith, Thomas (X) Woten
 - January Sessions This bill of sale was proven by the oath of Jesse Smith and Thomas Woten and ordered to be registered. [p396]

YEATMAN, Thomas   Deed of Trust   11 March 1820
I, John P. Erwin, convey to Thomas Yeatman the carriage and harness lately purchased by me from S. V. D. Stout. Thomas Yeatman is bound as endorser for me to the Branch Bank of Tennessee at Nashville and if the said sum of my debt shall be paid before the expiration of six months the said Yeatman will be discharged from all liability. 10 May 1820 Jno. P. Erwin Teste: John Catron
 - it is further agreed that said John P. Erwin keep the possession of said carriage and harness and have the use of it during the period of six months. Th Yeatman
 - May Term This deed of trust was acknowledged by John P. Erwin and ordered registered. [pp396/397]

SHUTE, John   Bill of Sale   11 May 1820
I, Thomas H. Fletcher, have sold to John Shute a certain stallion called *Waggoner*, aged about 9 years, the horse being the horse I bought of Benj. Wright. 12 Feb. 1820 Tho. H. Fletcher Teste G. G. Washington
 - April Sessions This bill of sale was proven by the oath of G. G. Washington

99

and ordered to be registered. [p397]

DREWRY, John   Bill of Sale   12 May 1820
I have this day sold to John Drewry a negro woman named Jeany, about fifty
years of age. 25 Feb. 1820   E. Dibrill
Teste: Duncan Robertson, Will. Howlett
- April Sessions This bill of sale was proven by the oath of Duncan 'Robertson
and William Howlett and ordered to be registered. [pp397/398]

CONDON, James   Bill of Sale   12 May 1820
I, William Arthur, have sold to James Condon the following property and articles
of household and kitchen furniture: two horses, one a bay and the other a sorrell,
one dray and all the gear and apperatus attached, one cart and harness, one gigg
and harness, four beds and furniture, one dozen of ornamented chairs, six
common chairs, one china press with all the furniture therein, one side board &
furniture, one closet and furniture, one sugar chest, three tables, 2 set of
andirons, one of brass, the other cast iron, two pair of shovel and tongs and
kitchen furniture of every description, 3 looking glasses. 29 Feb. 1820
Wm Arthur   Teste Will Scruggs, Thos H. Price
- April Sessions This bill of sale was proven by the oath of Willie Scruggs and
Thomas H. Price and ordered to be registered. [p398]

THOMPSON, John   Bill of Sale   13 May 1820
By virtue of two writs- the one issued by James Mulherrin, a Justice of the
Peace for the county of Davidson at the suit of Alexander Porter to me to charge
the goods of Henry Pasquit; the other issued by George Wilson, a Justice of the
Peace of Davidson, at the suit of Meridith Corbett against the goods and chattles
of John Newby and Henry Pasquit. I have seized and taken one negro woman
named Nancy, about the age of nineteen years and a negro boy named Peter
about the age of two years, the property of the said Henry Pasquit; Nancy and
Peter were exposed to sale at public vendue and purchased by John Thompson.
24 April 1820   Wm Howlett, Constable
- April Sessions This bill of sale was acknowledged by the said William
Howlett and ordered to be registered. [pp399/400]

CHILDRESS, John   Bill of Sale   20 May 1820
I, Jesse Charton, Administrator of the estate of William Wharton, deceased, have
sold to John Childress a negro man by the name of Robin, about twenty two or
three years of age, of a yellow complexion, being one of the negroes who came
into my possession as administrator and sold by an order of Davidson County
Court. 21 Nov. 1816 J. Wharton, Admr
- January Sessions 1817 This bill of sale was acknowledged in open court by
the said Jesse Wharton and ordered to be registered. [p400]

BIDEWELL, Charles   Bill of Sale   8 June 1820
We, Stephen Cantrell, Robert Searcy and Washington L. Hannum, for the
purpose of securing the payment of certain debts in the banks of Nashville [The
Nashville Bank, the Branch Bank of the State of Tennessee at Nashville and the
Farmers and Mechanics Bank of Nashville] due and owing said banks by John
Stump and John S. Cox, merchants and partners in trade under the firm of *Stump
& Cox* conveyed in trust to the said parties among other things several negroes
and the said parties did expose to auction on 19 Nov. 1819. Charles Bidwell did
become the purchaser of a negro boy named Jim. 2 December 1819
    Stephen Cantrell   Robt Searcy   Was. L. Hannum
Teste: John T. Dismukes, W. Barrow for W.L.H.
- May Term This bill of sale was acknowledged by Stephen Cantrell & Robert
Searcy and ordered certified. [pp400/401]

COOPER, Edmond   Deed of Trust   8 June 1820
I, Edwin Dibrell, have sold to Edmund Cooper the following described
household and kitchen furniture: 4 bedsteads, 4 beds, 12 blankets, 7 sheets, 1
press, 1 bureau, 2 tables, 9 chairs, 1 pair of looking glasses, 3 counterpanes, 1
carpet, 1 trunk, 1 chest, 1 cradle & cradle bed, 29 glasses, 10 cut glass tumblers,
2 cut glass decanters, 6 jelly glasses, 1 set castors, 2 pitchers, 7 silver
tablespoons, 1 dozen cups & saucers, 1 dozen dinner plates, 1 set of tea plates,
2 flowered decanters, 8 silver teaspoons, ovens, 2 skillets, 1 kettle, 1 pot, 5 pails,
2 smoothing irons, 1 rifle gun, 1 negro boy named Frank, 2 cows and calves and
1 silver watch. All of such furniture is now in the house of Edwin Dibrell on
Cherry Street in the city of Nashville and are hereby conveyed to the said
Edmond in trust for the said Edwin Dibrell is indebted to John Drewry and the
said John is security for notes to George Shall and John is also security for
Samuel Elam. If Edwin Dibrell shall pay such sums as due this deed of trust to
be void. 15 March 1820 E. Dibrell Edmd Copoper
Teste: J. P. Erwin, Williamson Adams
- April Sessions This deed of trust was acknowledged by the said Edwin
Dibrell and Edmond Cooper and ordered to be registered. [pp402/403]

KINGSBERRY, Joseph S.   Deed of Trust   28 June 1820
Gideon Gary, Jr. hereby sells to Joseph S. Kingsberry the following: a negro
female slave named Abby and her three children, Martha about eight years old,
Lucy about five or six years old, Mary about three years old; about 45 hogs, 3
horses, 1 gig, 2 cows and calves, about 2500 lbs bacon, about 200 lbs beef, 120
flour barrels, one bureau, 4 featherbeds, bedsteads & bedclothes, 4 tables, 20
windsor chairs, 1 candlestand, 1 cradle, 3 looking glasses, 1 pair   brass
andirons, 2 pair shovels and tongs, 1 cupboard, 1 mans saddle and 1 womans
saddle, 2 Martingills and 4 bridles, 1 settee, 1 set of Liverpool china [52 pieces]
2 stand castors, 4 pint decanters, 1 dozen wine glasses, 4 1/2 pine tumblers and

4 pint, 1 1/2 dozen Liverpool plates, 4 dishes, 2 teapots, 2 pitchers, 2 tea trays, 4 small waiters, 1/2 dozen silver tablespoons, 1 silver ladle, 1 sugar tong, 10 silver teaspoons, 2 brass candlesticks, 2 plated candlesticks, 1 old carpet, 10 knives & forks, 3 stone pots, 6 earthen pots, 1 10 gallon kettle, 2 small iron pots, 1 frying pan, 1 dutch oven, 1 skillet, 1 teakettle and 1 kitchen table, 5 tin pans, 1 2 dozen patterpans, 1/2 dozen tin cups, 1 coffeepot, 70 lb lard, 2 wash tables, 2 wooden cans, 1 tin bucket, 2 bread trays, 1 keel boat, 1 cart and a pair of oxen, 150 wt tallow, 1 wheelbarrow, 30 cords wood, 2 arm chairs, 2 maps, two guns, 1 pair saddle bags, 1 valice, about 70 or 80 plains, also all the books and all notes and accounts due to Gideon Gary & Co., also one undivided third part of 100 acres of land lying on poplar creek, land was purchased by Gary, Miller & McLemore. Gideon Gary & Co. executed two notes with Young Green & Co. as endorsers to J. Whiteside and Alfred Balch. One note due 1st January 1820 at the Branch Bank of the State of Tennessee at the instance of William Quarles the present holder for nonpayment ... said Young Green & Co as endorsers to J. Whiteside, A. Balch and E. S. Hall. 12 Feb. 1820   Gideon Gary, Jr.
Teste: W. Quarles, James Brown, Js Watson
- June Term Seventh Circuit District of West Tennessee I, Robert Searcy, Clerk of the Federal Circuit Court of the United States for the District of West Tennessee do hereby certify that the within deed of trust from Gideon Gary, Jr. to Joseph S. Kingsberry for the use of Jenkin Whiteside and Alfred Balch was proven in open court by Wm Quarles and James Watson and ordered to be certified for registration. [pp404/405/406]

PRYOR, Nicholas B.   Bill of Sale   13 July 1820
I, Samuel Elam, have sold to Nicholas B. Pryor the following negro slaves: Peggy, aged about twenty eight years, and her seven children, Julia, Tom, Sally, Martha, Davy, Patrick and Emily. The seven children are from the age of twelve down to less than one year of age. 18 Jan. 1820   Sam. Elam
Test: M. S. Gross, D. A. C. Hayes
- January Sessions This bill of sale was proven by the oath of M. S. Gross and D. A. C. Hays and ordered to be registered. [pp406/407]

HARPER, William   Deed of Trust   11 August 1820
William Garner has this day sold to William Harper the following articles to secure Duncan Robertson, Samuel V. D. Stout and John Tolevill as endorsers for said William Garner and to secure the payment of debt to Nathan Ewing: one side board with pedestals, 12 windsor chairs, a settee, a bureau, 4 featherbeds, 15 half worn blankets of the point and rose kind, 1 bedstead, high posted with teasters, one low bedstead, 2 iron pots, 1 skillet, 1 teakettle, 2 dozen knives & forks, 1/2 dozen silver teaspoons, one and a half dozen common table and teaspoons, two dozen delph plates, 4 dishes of various sizes, 2 teapots, 1 coffeepot ^ boiler, 6 pair of sheets, six quilts, 2 washing tubs, 2 pails, 2 piggins,

a thousand feet of cherry plank 1/4 thick, three hundred feet of cherry plank 1/2 thick, one receipt of Matthew Porters for cherry timber, the residue of timber not levied upon by Thos. Hickman, one sideboard part finished, two Madison tables part finished, two breakfast tables part finished, one bedstead part finished, one tin plate stove, one lowposted poplar bedstead, one pilas? & elm breakfast table, one Jackson press part finished, one bureau, part finished. In Trust - if debts are not paid within twelve months from this date the sale shall proceed. 7 July 1820
      Wm Garner   Teste: Henry Long, M. Monahan
- July Sessions This deed of trust was proven in open court by the oath of Henry Long and M. Monahan and ordered to be registered. [pp407/408]

BARROW, Willie   Deed of Trust   12 August 1820
I, Pleasant Craddock, have sold to Willie Barrow the following negroes: Daniel, a man aged about thirty five or forty years; Bob, about twenty seven; Frank, about twenty; Frederick, about eighteen; Charles, about fourteen; Sarah, about thirty; Nancy about fourteen; Mariah, about fifteen; Fanny , about thirty. Whereas Charles Warfield of Baltimore by his attorney Henry Crabb did on the 24th day of October 1818 obtain a judgement against me in the County Court of Davidson County. If debt is paid as agreed this deed to be void but if Craddock fail to pay it shall be the duty of the said Willie to take possession of as many negroes as will be sufficient to pay the amount due. It is understood that said negroes although possession thereof is not delivered to said Willie are to be returned into the service of said Craddock at his tavern. 28 June 1820
    Pleasant Craddock   Teste: Kendal Webb, Hugh Keys
- July Sessions This deed of trust was proven by the oath of Kendal Webb and Hugh Keys and ordered to be registered. [pp409/410]

BLACKMAN, Bennet   Deed of Trust   14 August 1820
John Blackman is indebted to several persons and many judgments have been rendered against him and Bennet Blackman has become security for John therefore this Indenture made 5 April 1819 from John Blackman, Jr. to Bennet Blackman. John Blackman does sell the following property: one negro man named Robin between thirty and forty years of age; one negro woman named Jude, upwards of sixty years of age, one stud horse called *Sir William*.
    John Blackman   Teste: Stephen Blackman, Charlotte Joyce
- July Sessions This deed of trust was proven in open court by the oath of Stephen Blackman and Charlotte Joyce and ordered registered. [pp411/412]

BLACKMAN, Bennet   Deed of Trust   14 August 1820
Benjamin Turbiville is indebted to several persons, particularly to W. Philips for a waggon and team, and Bennet Blackman has become security. In Trust - I sell to B. Blackman the following property: one wagon and four horses, four pair of wagon harness, including the wagon, horses and gears the said Turbiville

103

purchased from William Philips. 18 Dec. 1818 Benj. Turbiville
Teste: Stephen Blackman, Henry Ewing
- July Sessions This deed of trust was acknowledged by Benja. Turbiville and
ordered to be registered. [pp412/413]

HINTON, John J. and William M.   Bill of Sale   14 August 1820
I, George W. Boyd, have sold to John J. and William M. Hinton a negro woman
and three children: Paul is about thirty five years old, Charity is about fifteen
years old, Ellender is about three years old and Abraham is one year, 8 months
old. 14 July 1820   G. W. Boyd   Teste: Jno Hobson, John McGavock
- July Sessions This bill of sale was acknowledged by George W. Boyd as his
act and deed and ordered to be registered. [p413]

HINTON, John   Bill of Sale   14 August 1820
I have sold to John Hinton a negro boy by the name of Alfred, aged about
fourteen years old. Price paid to Robertson & Curry, Auctioneers of the town
of Nashville. 17 May 1820   John Boyd
Test: J. Currey, Tho. Young, R. H. Barry
- July Sessions This bill of sale was proven by the oath of J. Currey and Richard
H. Barry and ordered to be registered. [pp413/414]

HINTON, William M.   Bill of Sale   14 August 1820
I, John Boyd, for cash paid to Duncan Robertson and Currey, Auctioneers in the
Town of Nashville I have sold to William M. Hinton a negro boy slave by the
name of Oliver, aged about twelve years old. 17 May 1820 Jno Boyd
Test: J. Currey, John Hinton
- July Sessions This bill of sale was proven by the oath of J. Currey and John
Hinton and ordered to be registered. [p414]

EAKINS, Rebecca   Deed of Mortgage   14 August 1820
I, John Hopper, have sold to Rebecca Eakins the following property: one mare
and colt, one saddle and bridle. If debt is paid this deed to be void. 27 June 1820
John Hopper   Teste: Tho. H. Baker, Patty Eakins (X) her mark
- July Sessions This deed of mortgage was acknowledged by John Hopper and
ordered to be registered. [pp415/416]

FRAZOR, Rebecca   Articles of Agreement   14 August 1820
Whereas by the laws of the State of Tennessee where a person dying intestate
shall leave more than two children his widow is only entitled to a childs part of
the personal estate.   And whereas Daniel Frazor, having departed this life
without making a last will and Testament leaving a widow, Rebecca Frazor, and
nine children namely - Sally Childress, John Frazor, Moses B. Frazor, William
Frazor, James Frazor, Ebenezer Frazor, Daniel Frazor, Emeline M. Dickson and

Stephen D. Frazor and it appearing to the above named children of the said Daniel Frazor deceased that a childs part of the personal estate of the deceased will be inadequate to the support and maintenance of their mother, Rebecca Frazor, in the style and manner she has hitherto been accustomed and the said Rebecca Frazor, widow and relict of Daniel Frazor deceased not only being willing but preferring to take and receive one third part of the personal estate of her late husband for and during the term of her natural life only, or widowhood, it is hereby agreed by and between the said Rebecca Frazor and Reps O. Childress for himself and his wife Sally Childress, John Frazor, Moses B. Frazor, William Frazor by his next friend Ebenezer Frazor, James Frazor, Ebenezer Frazor, Daniel Frazor by his next friend James Frazor, John M. For himself and wife Emiline M. Dickson and Stephen D. Frazor by his next friend Moses B. Frazor that in consideration of the premises and for as much as the said Rebecca doth hereby relinquish in behalf of her above named children all right and title which she may have under the law to a childs part of the personal estate of her deceased husband Daniel Frazor they do hereby relinquish all right and interest they may have in and to one third part of the personal estate in behalf of their said mother for and during her natural life or widowhood. 8 Oct. 1819

Rebecca Frazor   Reps O. Childress   Moses B. Frazor   John Frazor
Ebenezer Frazor   for   William Frazor   James Frazor   Ebenezer Frazor
James Frazor   for   Daniel Frazor   John M. Dickson
Moses B. Frazor   for   Stephen D. Frazor
Teste: Jacob Dickinson, George Frazor

- October Sessions 1819 The within articles of agreement was proven in open Court by the oath of Jacob Dickinson and ordered to be certified. [pp416, 417, 418]

MOORE, James [agent for Thomas Ramsey] Bill of Sale   22 August 1820
I, Lott Hazard of Smith County and State of Tennessee have sold to James Moore, agent for Thomas Ramsey, a negro man named Stephen, about twenty two years old. 25 July 1820   Lot Hazard
- July Sessions This bill of sale was acknowledged by Lott Hazard and ordered registered. [p418]

McLENDON, Dennis   Bill of Sale   22 August 1820
We have sold to Dennis McLendon a negro boy about fifteen years of age, named Sam. 28 Jan. 1820Wm P. Campbell   James Campbell
Teste: P. W. Campbell, John Huggins
- April Sessions This bill of sale was acknowledged by William P. and James to be their act and ordered to be registered. [p419]

YEATMAN, Thomas   Deed of Trust   23 August 1820
I, John P. Erwin convey to Thomas Yeatman a negro woman named Claret, aged

about forty years. Thomas Yeatman is bound as endorser on my note to the Branch Bank of the State of Tennessee at Nashville. If said note is paid by me then this conveyance to be void. 28 July 1820 John P. Erwin
- July Sessions This deed of trust was acknowledged by John P. Erwin and ordered to be registered. [pp419/420]

ERWIN, John P.   Article of Agreement   23 August 1820
This agreement made 7 August 1820 between Robert Searcy and John P. Erwin; Viz: on 9 June 1820 Robert Searcy by his agent purchased at Marshalls sale the following property taken in execution on the property of John P. Erwin: one negro boy hamed Thomas, 1 girl, Maria; 1 boy, Squire and one girl child, Rose; 1 pianoforte, 1 violin, 1 clock and mantle ornaments, 1 bookcase, 2 card tables, 1 ink stand, 1 small writing desk, 1 large chair, 1 music stool, 2 doz windsor chairs, 1 new carpet, sundry music books and pieces of music, 1 pr looking glasses, 6 pictures, sundry books, [1 set encyclopedia - 20 vols, Rollins *Ancient History*, 8 Vols Shakespears plays, 8 Vols. *Massachusetts Reports*, 14 Vols Bacon *Abridgement*, 7 Vols. *Branches Reports,* 9 Vols. *American Law Journal,* 6 Vols *American Digest*, 2 Vol. Chitty *Pleadings*, 3 Vols. *Criminal Law,* 4 Vols Comyn on *Contracts*, 2 Vols Jacob Law Dictionary, 1 large Bible, Ten Reports, 2 Vol. Douglass *Reports*, 2 Vols. Roberts on *Frauds,* 1 Vol. Blackstones *Commentaries*, 4 Vol. Easts *Reports*, 16 Vols Mitford on *Plees,* 1 Vol Tidds *Practice*, sundry other books named in act. of sales - also 1 pr andirons, shovel and tongs, fenders, 4 beds, bedsteads, clothing etc., 1 Bureau, 1 Secretary, 1 Press, Sundry glass and chinaware, knives & forks, spoons, Queensware, kitchen furniture, set dining tables, glass ware etc as will appear by reference. Searcy is willing to permit John P. Erwin to make use of said property as done when owned by himself.   Robt Searcy   Jno. P. Erwin
Witness: Geo. S. Yerger, R. W. Williams
- United States of America District of West Tennessee I, Robert Searcy, Clerk of the Circuit Court of the United States for West Tennessee District certifies that the within Article of Agreement was proven by the oaths of Geo. S. Yerger and R. W. Williams and ordered to be so certified. 7 Aug. 1820
    Robt Searcy Clk by J. P. Ervin Dep. [pp420/421]

CROW, William L.   Bill of Sale   5 Sept 1820
I James Crow, sell to William L. Crow three horses, ten cattle, eighteen sheep, sixteen hogs, all I now own, and one wagon with four pair of harness and all farming utensils. James (X) Crow   Test: John L. Cobler, Henry Stobaugh
- July Sessions This bill of sale was acknowledged by James Crow to be his act and deed and ordered to be registered. [pp421/422]

McNAIRY, John   Deed of Trust   12 Nov. 1820
I, Thomas Eastland, have sold to John McNairy the following described negroes:
Howard, a negro man aged about twenty, about five feet, five to seven inches;
also one mulato boy named Ned, about twelve years; Martha, a negro woman
aged about twenty eight; Sally, commonly called Gibson, aged about twenty
eight years & Daniel, a son of Sally, aged about seven years, also an infant two
or three months old, a child of Sally; one dark chestnut sorrel horse, being the
horse I purchased from Doctr John Shelby in 1818. In Trust - I am indebted to
James Stewart, Marshall & Watkins, merchants of Nashville are endorsers; also
indebted to the Farmers & Mechanics Bank of Nashville, also the Branch Bank
of the State of Tennessee at Nashville, Doctr Boyd McNairy endorser. Eastland
shall keep the possession of said property for two years and if debts are not paid
at that time it is to be advertised for sale. 26 Jan. 1820 Thos. Eastland
 - January Sessions This Deed of Trust was acknowledged by Thomas Eastland
and ordered to be registered. [pp422/423/424]

MOOREMAN, Polly   Bill of Sale   16 Nov. 1820
I, Thomas Patteson, have sold to Polly Mooreman a negro man slave called
Dave, aged twenty three years. 16 Feb. 1820   Thomas Patteson
 Test: John Hughs, William H. (X) Young
 - October Sessions This bill of sale was acknowledged by Thomas Patteson and
ordered to be registered. [p424]

MOREMAN, Polly   Bill of Sale   16 Nov. 1820
I, Thomas Patteson, have sold to Polly Moreman a negro man slave called Bill,
of the age of nineteen years. 4 March 1820 Thomas Patteson
Test: David T. Hatch, Warner Loving, Samuel Nicerline
 - October Sessions This bill of sale was acknowledged by Thomas Patteson and
ordered registered. [p425]

HARDING, Thomas & David   Bill of Sale   16 Nov. 1820
John Harding held in trust for Thomas and David M. Harding [then minors]
certain negroes belonging to the estate of Giles Harding, dec'd named Ned,
Jenny, Isaac, Polly & Peggy to go to them when they became of lawful age. Now
in discharge of the Trust I do transfer and set over to Thomas and David M.
Harding the negroes above named. 25 May 1816 Jno Harding
Test: Jacob Thompson
 - October Sessions This bill of sale was acknowledged by John Harding and
ordered to be registered. [pp425/426]

BAKER, James   Bill of Sale   16 Nov. 1820
I, John Drewry, sell to James Baker one negro child named Biddy, about three
years old. 17 Oct. 1820   John Drewry   Test: A. M. Harwood, Susan Adams

- October Sessions This bill of sale was acknowledged by John Drewry and ordered to be registered. [p426]

GIBBS, George W.　　　　Deed of Trust　　　　16 Nov. 1820
Roger B. Sappington is indebted to John H. Lewis and has this day sold to George W. Gibbs three negro men slaves; Abram, aged thirty; Jeem, about thirty or thirty five and Bentley, aged about twenty five or thirty years. The said negroes are to remain in possession of Roger B. Sappington until March 1, 1821. If debt is paid before that date this deed to be void. 18 May 1820
　Roger B. Sappington　　　Attest: Simon Glenn, Andrew Hays
 - July Sessions This deed of trust was proven by the oath of Simon Glenn and ordered to be certified.
 - October Sessions This deed of trust was proven by the oath of Andrew Hays and ordered to be registered. [pp426/427]

HARDGRAVE, John　　　　Bill of Sale　　　　16 Nov. 1820
I, John Demoss, do this day sell to John Hardgrave a negro man named Harry, about twenty eight years of age. Harry is now in the State of Louisiana and supposed to be in possession of Skelton Hardgraves. 15 July 1820
　　John Demoss　　　　　　　Test: Jno. Davis
 - October Sessions This bill of sale was acknowledged by John Demoss to be his act and deed and ordered to be registered. [p428]

HARDGRAVE, John　　　　Bill of Sale　　　　17 Nov. 1820
I, Samford Coil of the State of Georgia and County of Burk, have sold to John Hardgrave a negro man by the name of Jesse, between the age of twenty four and twenty six. 16 Feb. 1819　Sanford Coil　Teste: G. B. Taylor, John Demoss
 - October Sessions This bill of sale was proven by the oath of G. B. Taylor and John Demoss and ordered to be registered. [p428]

NICHOLS, John　　　　Bill of Sale　　　　17 Nov. 1820
I, Greenwood Payne, have this day sold by virtue of twelve executions all the right, title and claim that Alfred Nichols had or has to twenty one negroes for the fifth part of said twenty one negroes, his part of the estate of John Nichols deceased; to wit - Reuben, Ben, Dennis, Ryal, Jordon, Sally, Siller, Delilah, Reuben, Alliss, Sally, Tom, Noah, Anica, John, Bob, Wilson, York, Jacob, Edmond, Israel; also one sorrel horse, his own property and two cattle and John Nichols being the highest bidder for the negroes . April 26, 1820
　　　Greenwood Payne　　　Test: Jas. Carter
 - October Sessions This bill of sale was proven by the oath of James Carter and ordered to be certified. [p429]

SCRUGGS, Langhorn   Bill of Sale   17 Nov. 1820
I, Eli Talbot, have sold to Langhorn Scruggs a negro boy slave named Joe, about twelve years. 1 July 1819   E. Talbot
- This bill of sale was acknowledged by Eli Talbot to be his act and deed and ordered to be registered. [p429]

SHALL, George   Deed of Trust   18 Nov. 1820
Zachariah Waters has executed to Thomas Claiborne his note drawn payable to George Hicks and indorsed by Hicks and by Howland and Allen. To secure said note Waters does sell to Stephen Cantrell and George Shall one mulatto negro girl slave named Dinah aged about thirteen years, one negro girl slave named Betty, aged about six years and one negro boy named Randle, aged about six years. The slaves shall remain in the possession of the said Zachariah. If the note is not paid the slaves may be sold upon proper notice and advertisement. 2 October 1819 Z. W. Waters   Stephen Cantrell   Geo. Shall
Attest: Robt Bradford
- April Sessions This deed of trust was proven by the oath of Robert Bradford and ordered to be registered.   [pp430/431]

OVERTON, John   Deed of Trust   18 Nov. 1820
I, James Mulherrin, have sold to John Overton all the negroes following: a negro woman named Sarah, aged twenty five; Moriah, a girl aged ten years and six months; Nancy, a girl aged nine years; Bedford, a boy aged seven; Lauinia, a girl aged five years; Eliazer, a boy aged three years; Julianna, a girl one year and four months, all named after Sarah are children of Sarah. In Trust - James Mulherrin did on the 24th of February 1814 execute his note to John Buchanon, which is now due and payable. If James Mulherrin shall pay the debt and interest in twenty four months from this date then this deed to be void. 6 Oct. 1820
                    James Mulherrin   Test: Thomas H. Everett
- October Sessions This deed of trust was acknowledged by James Mulherrin to be his act and deed and ordered to be registered. [pp431/432/433]

MARTIN, William   Bill of Sale   2 Dec. 1820
I, Stephen Cantrell, have sold to William Martin of Smith County in Tennessee negro Tom, about twenty years of age of dark complexion; negro girl Sarah, about eighteen years of age of dark complexion; her child about 5 months old, named Major; Ben, about thirteen years old, of dark complexion. 7 Oct. 1820
                    Steph'n Cantrell   Test: Ephraim H. Foster, William Boggs
- Nov. Term   This bill of sale was acknowledged by Stephen Cantrell and ordered registered. [p433]

THOMPSON, William   Deed of Trust   8 Dec. 1820
Willie Barrow has sold to William Thompson the following negroes: one negro

boy named Traviss, about ten years old; a mulatto boy named Caswell, about thirteen years; a negro boy named Bill, about seven years old; a negro woman named Milley, about fifty years old; a negro girl named Caroline, of black colour, aged about nine. In Trust - if debt is paid this deed to be void - said negroes are to continue in the possession of the said Willie. 20 Nov. 1820

W. Barrow   Test: Felix Robertson, Peyton Robertson

- Nov. Term This mortgage was acknowledged and ordered to be registered. [p434]

FOSTER, Ephraim H.   Deed of Trust   1 Jan. 1821
I, William Davis, have sold to Ephraim H. Foster the following negro slaves; Joe, a negro man of dark complexion, about 23 years of age; Frederic, a negro boy of dark colour, about sixteen years of age; Moses a negro boy of dark complexion about 15 years of age and Bob, a negro man of yellow complexion about 21 years of age. In Trust - William Davis has executed his bond to Enoch Douge with William Lytle and Daniel A. Dunham as securities. If at any time Lytle and Dunham have in consequence of said notes loss, Davis binds himself and gives to Foster authority to take possession of all or either of said negroes conveyed to be sold to repay them any monies they have advanced for Davis ... If Davis shall pay debts as they become due this deed to become void.
21 March 1820 William Davis   Test: John S. Topp, M. Barrow
- May Term 1820 This deed of trust was proven by the oaths of John S. Topp and Matthew Barrow and ordered to be registered. [pp435/436

FOSTER, Ephraim H.   Deed of Trust   1 Jan. 1821
Whereas George Shall and Daniel A. Dunham are bound as endorsers for William Davis on notes to the Branch Bank of the State of Tennessee at Nashville, and the Farmers & Mechanics Bank for Nashville and whereas William Davis is indebted to George Shall, Davis is willing to secure the said Shall and Dunham , William and Davis assigns the following negro slaves; Boliver, of dark complexion about thirty years of age and his wife Chloe of dark complexion, about twenty five years old and Tom, their child of black complexion five years old, and Moses their child of black complexion, three years old. Davis also makes over the following debts due and owing by the individuals hereinafter mentioned: judgment recovered in the name of said Davis against James N. Mannifee and judgment obtained in my name by the Circuit Court of Rutherford county against James Childress on a note executed by Childress to John P. Erwin & Co; judgment obtained against Thomas Saunders. If notes are paid this conveyance to be void. Wm Davis
Test: John S. Topp, M. Barrow
- The annexed Deed of Trust proven by the oaths of John S. Topp and Matthew Barrow and ordered registered. [pp437-440]

McLAUGHLIN, William H.   Bill of Sale   2 Jan. 1821
I, James McLaughlin, do sell a nigress named Elenor, about twenty five years of age to William H. McLaughlin. 21 October 1821   Jas McLaughlin
Test: Jno C. Rea
- October Sessions This bill of sale proven by the oath of John C. Rea and ordered registered. [p440]

CHAPMAN, John   Bill of Sale   9 Feb. 1821
Alexander McDowell has sold to John Chapman a negro man named Henry, about twenty three years of age. 29 Dec. 1817   Alex'r McDowell
Test: Geo. Smith
- Nov. Sessions This bill of sale was proven by the oath of George Smith and ordered registered. [pp440/441]

COOTS, John   Bill of Sale   12 Feb. 1821
I, Sarah Davis, Executrix of the last will of William Davis, deceased, have sold to John Coots a negro slave named Lige, about twenty three years old of black colour. 11 October 1820 Sarah (X) Davis, executrix
Test: Henry Crabb, Jo. H. Talbot
- October Sessions This bill of sale was proven by the oath of Henry Crabb and Joseph H. Talbot and ordered to be registered. [p441]

ELLISTON, John   Bill of Sale   12 Feb. 1821
We, George Crockett and Thomas P. Adams, acting under the firm of Crockett and Adams in the Town of Nashville, have sold to John Elliston a certain female mulatto slave called Maria, about the age of fifteen years. 20 Nov. 1820 George Crockett Thos P. Adams   Test: Will Lytle, J. O. Cummins
- January Sessions This bill of sale was proven by the oath of William Lytle and T. O. Cummins[p442]

FOSTER, Ephraim H.   Deed of Trust   12 Feb. 1821
I, John Drewry, do sell to E. H. Foster all the negroes following: James, Jane and her three children, George, Parnham & Julia. In Trust - John Drewry did execute a note to John Fitzhugh - also a credit paid to Robert Buchanon for John Buchanon; Also a note to John Buchanon. If John Drury shall pay the amount of balance and interest this deed to be void. 13 Dec. 1820 Jno. Drewry
Test: E. Dibrell, Edmund H. Foss
- January Sessions This deed of trust was acknowledged by the said Drewry to be his act and deed and ordered to be registered. [pp442/443]

GLEAVES, Michael   Bill of Sale   12 Feb. 1821
I, George Tunstall, have sold a certain negro boy, aged eight years, named Bristoe, to Michael Gleaves. 23 Jan. 1821   Geo. Tunstall

Test: J. Norvell, M. S. Gross
- January Sessions This bill of sale was acknowledged by the said George Tunstall to be his act and deed and ordered to be registered. [p444]

HARRIS, Howell   Bill of Sale   12 Feb. 1821
I, William Harris, have sold the following negroes to Howell Harris: a negro woman named Rhoda about forty five years old; a negro woman named Nancy about twenty five years old; a negro woman named Dinah about thirty five years old; one negro boy named Kinchen about twelve years old; one negro boy named Little Ben about eight years old; Philip a negro boy about eight years; George a negro boy six years old; Jacob, about four years old; Grigsby, a boy about three years old; a boy named Antoney about two years old; one negro child about five months old named Viney. Nov. 8, 1820   William Harris
- January Sessions This bill of sale was acknowledged by William Harriss to be his act and deed and ordered to be registered. [pp444/445]

BRYLEY, John   Bill of Sale   12 Feb. 1821
I, Aaron Murphey, sell to John Bryley the following property: one lease for about seventeen acres of land where said Murphy now lives for the balance of his time, one cow & yearling, 1 bed and furniture, one spinning wheel, one set of knives and forks, one set earthern plates, one dish, one mans saddle, one iron pot and skillet. 24 January 1821   Aaron Murphey
- January Sessions This bill of sale was acknowledged by the said Aron Murphey to be his act and deed and ordered to be registered. [p445]

LUCAS, Isaac   Deed of Mortgage   13 Feb. 1821
I, Absalom Hooper, sell to Isaac Lucas the following described negro slaves: negro man Caesar, light complexion about 52 years old; negro man Bill, dark complexion about 24 years old; negro Sam of dark complexion about 20 years of age; negro boy Ben of light complexion aged 9 years; negro girl Peg of black complexion 4 years old; negro girl Clary of dark complexion aged 19 years; negro woman Winney of light complexion about 26 years of age; Winneys three childred, Elijah of light colour aged 8, Claiborne aged 5 years, Sintha aged 3 years; negro woman Mary about 27 years of dark complexion and her child Julia, an infant. If said Hooper pays his debt with interest this deed to be void.
14 December 1820 A. Hooper   Test: J. Hooper, Eli Lucas
- January Sessions This Deed of Mortgage was acknowledged by Absolom Hooper to be his act and deed and ordered to be registered. [pp446/447]

OWEN, William P.   Bill of Sale   13 Feb. 1821
I, James W. Glasgow, have sold to William P. Owen of the County of Madison and State of Alabama, seven negro slaves: Patty, Ned, Alfred, Charlotte, Jim, Edmund & Tempe, which negroes are now in the possession of Bennet

Blackman. 26 Nov. 1819   Jas. W. Glasgow
Test: Clarinda Glasgow, C. Goodrich, George W. Charlton
- January Sessions This bill of sale was proven by the oath of C. Goodrich and George W. Charlton and ordered to be registered. [p447]

HOOPER, Absalom   Bill of Sale   22 Feb. 1821
I, Nimrod Hooper of Jefferson County and State of Mississippi, have this day sold to Absalom Hooper of the county and state aforesaid, one negro boy named Andrew, aged 37 years. 17 March 1819 N. Hooper
Test: John Lucas, Eli Lucas
- July Sessions This bill of sale was proven by the oath of John Lucas and Eli Lucas and ordered to be registered. [448]

FOSTER & NORVELL   Deed of Mortgage   24 Feb. 1821

In consideration of debt due E. H. Foster and Joseph Norvell I hereby convey the aforesaid Foster and Norvell my interest and claim to the following articles: one cherry press, one press for *Seyen*, one large folding table on rollers, one small folding table, eighteen green and grown windsor chairs, one candle stand, two *pin* glasses, gilt frames, two pair cut glass Decanters, one pair castors silver bands, one pair plated candlesticks, one pair brass candlesticks, tumblers and wine glasses, cut glass, two dozen Ivory handled knives and forks with carvers, one set case knives and forks and steel, two dozen large blue plates, four dishes, two dishes, one sauce boat, china teacups and saucers, tea pats, etc., one bread basket, one large and two small waiters, two snuffers and trays, one ladle, one pair cut glass salts, one set table matts, two large canisters, one black tin coffeepot, one coffeemill, four pitchers, one pair brass and one pair metal andirons, sundry pots, ovens, potrack, shovel & tongs. pails, tubs, teakettle, iron frying pan, etc, five pr large rose blankets, five pr linen sheets, two feather beds, two bedsteads, bellows and brushes, one portable desk, one chest drawers and secretary, one dressing glass with marble slab, one walnut cot, one set Nicholsons Encyclopedia in 12 vols, one set Dublin Edition in 18 vols, Plutarch *Lives*, 2 Bibles, etc., one Dearborn wagon, one saddle & bridle, 4 trunks, sundry empty barrels, etc. If payment is made within twelve months the above conveyance to be void. 18 Jan. 1821 Jas W. McLaughlin
- January Sessions This deed of mortgage was acknowledged by James McLaughlin and ordered to be registered. [pp448/449]

ROBERTSON, Eldridge B.   Bill of Sale   3 April 1821
I, Washington L. Hannum, have this day sold and delivered to Eldridge B. Robertson five negro slaves: Daniel, aged thirty five years; Rachael, aged forty; Moria, aged thirteen; Levi, aged eight; Milley, aged four and one half. 30 March 1821   Was. L. Hannum   Test: Nathan Ewing, Wm Quarles

Quarles and ordered to be registered.[p449]

HYDE, Edmund   Bill of Sale   17 May 1821
We, Stephen Cantrell, Robert Searcy and Washington L. Hannum of the one part
and Edmond Hyde of the other part -- For the purpose of securing the payment
of certain debts to The Nashville Bank, To the Branch Bank of the State of
Tennessee at Nashville and to the Farmers & Mechanics Bank of Nashville by
John Stump and John S. Cox, merchants in trade under the firm and style of
Stump and Cox, said John Stump by his indenture bearing date 23 March 1819
conveyed in trust to the parties of the first part among other things several
negroes AND the parties of the first part by the authority vested in them due
notice being given did expose on 19th of November 1819 among other things
the negroes of said Stump and Cox. At which time E. Hyde did become the
purchaser of a negro girl Feriby. 29 Feb. 1820
          Stephen Cantrell   Was. L. Hannum
- January Sessions This bill of sale was acknowledged by Stephen Cantrell and
Washington L. Hannum to be their act and deed and ordered to be registered.
[pp450/451]

HAYWOOD, George W., Martha & Egbert   Bill of Sale   17 May 1821
I, John Haywood, for and in consideration of the natural love and affection I have
and bear unto my loving and affectionate wife Martha, to hereby give and assign
all my claim to two negroes, Henry and Mary; And to Geo W. Haywood in trust
for and to the use of the said Martha for and during the term of her natural life.
15 Jan. 1820   J. Haywood   Test: H. W. Collier, Clem Hall
And after the death of said Martha Haywood the said negroes and increase shall
belong to and be the property of Egbert Haywood, her son, forever.
    J. Haywood   G. W. Haywood   Test: Clem Hall, H. W. Collier
- July Sessions 1820 This bill of sale proven by the oath of Clem Hall and H.
W. Collier and ordered to be registered. [p452]

COOPER, Edmond   Deed of Trust   17 May 1821
I, John M. Hill, in consideration of the sum of $539.25 by John Drewry and also
the further sum of one dollar paid by Edmund Cooper, I have sold to the said
Edmund Cooper the following described articles, one half of which belongs to
the above named John Drewry and only one half to myself: one waggon, five
horses and gears two ... a cart, and a boat 64 foot long built for the purpose of
boating wood down and the hire of a negro man named Pollydore belonging to
the estate of widow Wilkinson and all the firewood that is cut on the land of
Severn Donelson at the mouth of Stones River, and are hereby conveyed to the
said Edmond Cooper. Whereas John M. Hill is indebted to the said John Drewry
... if Hill shall pay this sale to be void. 25 April 1821   Jno M. Hill
- April Sessions This deed of trust was acknowledged by John M. Hill and

114

ordered to be registered. [pp452-454]

WILLIAMS, Robert   Bill of Sale   17 May 1821
Sold to Robert Williams a negro woman named Priscilla and her child, Elvira.
15 Feb. 1821   Neal Hopkins   Attest: Solomon L. Holder, Joel Johns
- April Sessions This bill of sale was proven by the oath of Solomon L. Holder
and Joel Johns and ordered to be registered. [p454]

MILLER, William S.   Bill of Sale   17 May 1821
I have sold to William S. Miller a certain negro woman by the name of Sabe and
her child Minerva aged about twenty two and child about three. 25 July 1820
     John Donly   Test: Alex Waites
- April Sessions This bill of sale was acknowledged by John Donley to be his
act and ordered to be registered. [pp454/455]

FRAZIER, Moses B.   Bill of Sale   17 May 1821
I, John M. Dixon, have sold to Moses B. Frazier two small negroes; Jean, aged
about eleven years and Alfred, aged about eight. 29 August 1820   John M.
Dickson Test: S. C. McDaniel, Cyreneo Emmons
 - This bill of sale was proven by the oath of S. C. McDaniel and Cyreneo
Emmons and ordered to be registered. [p455]

FRAZOR, Rebeccah   Bill of Sale   18 May 1821
I, Daniel M. Frazor, sell to Rebeccah Frazor one small negro girl, Luiza, aged
about three years old. 5 April 1821   Daniel M. Frazier
Test: Willis Swann, M. B. Frazier
- This bill of sale was proven by the oath of Willis Swann and M. B. Frazier and
ordered to be registered. [p456]

NORVELL, Moses   Deed of Trust   18 May 1821
Thomas Hill is indebted to the Nashville Bank, notes endorsed by Jenken
Whitesides, Alfred Balch and David Cummins, John Bosley & Robert Hill, Jno
Bosley & Felix Robertson, Moses Norvell and S. V. D. Stout, and to secure debt
does convey to Moses Norvell the following property: a negro man named
Davey, a drayman, Chloe, his wife and Davy, Mary Ann and Albert, their
children, being the family of negroes now in the possession of said Tho. Hill;
also a mulatto girl named Winney, aged about eighteen or twenty, being the same
that was willed by the late Jesse W. Thomas, dec'd, to the said Tho Hills wife
and also in the possession of said Thos. Hill. Also all the household and kitchen
furniture of the said Tho Hills of every description; four beds and bedsteads, a
mattress, bed furniture of blankets, sheets, counterpains and curtains, a bureau
and bookcase with the books therein, two other bureaus, a sugar chest, work

table, childs crib and furniture belonging thereto, a sideboard, all the glass, china a Delfware, knives and forks, candle sticks, snufflers, shovels and tongs and irons, both brass and iron, tables, chairs, carpets, a pair of large gilt frame looking glasses, one add. dressing glasses as well, also a counting room desk, a dray cart, two dray horses, a cow and calf, an armed writing chair and also a large keelboat now lying on the island below town. If said Thomas Hill shall pay said notes this indenture shall be void. 6 Sept. 1820 Th. Hill
John L. Allen   J. O. Cummins Sept 11, 1820
- This deed of trust was proven by the oath of John L. Allen and John O. Cummins and ordered to be registered. [pp456-458]

TALBOT, Thomas   Deed of Trust   18 May 1821
Eli Talbot did on the 23rd day of December 1819 execute his note to Thomas Talbot, payable in sixty days to the Farmers and Mechanics Bank of Nashville, endorsed by Thomas Talbot and Felix Robertson, since renewed and the Farmers and Mechanics Bank are also holders of a Bill of Exchange drawn by the said Eli Talbot on Breedlove, Bradford and Robeson of New Orleans, endorsed by Thomas Talbot. In consideration of the payments of the above by Thomas Talbot the said Eli Talbot does convey to Thomas Talbot the following effects: one negro woman, Priscilla, aged about forty years, one bay horse, one sorrell horse, 160 acres of land lying in Madison County, Alabama near New Market, about fifteen miles from Huntsville, being the same which Eli Talbot purchased of Thomas B. Smith in exchange of payment to debts outstanding to George Smith of Madison County, Alabama; Robert S. Browning of said county for the conveyance of three lots in the town of New Market; also James G. Hicks obligation for the conveyance of eight hundred acres of land lying in Barren County, Kentucky, dated 22 June 1819; also a bond given by George Hicks and James G. Hicks to said Eli Talbot dated 30 Sept 1819 for the conveyance of 200 acres of land in Barren County, Kentucky, to be performed when the said Eli shall have paid to L---ry Bishop a certain sum of money, said bond now in the office of the clerk of Barren County Clerk; also an obligation of John Perkins given to Isaac and George Chandler and by them assigned to John Garner and by said Garner sold to the said Eli Talbot dated 25 Nov. 1816 for the conveyance of 200 acres of land in Warren County, Kentucky; also a note given by Joseph D. Smith to said Eli Talbot on which suit has been brought in Limestone County, Alabama; notes are secured by a deed of mortgage executed by the said James G. Hicks to the said Eli Talbot for seven negroes therein mentioned dated 30 Sept. 1819, and which said deed of mortgage are hereby assigned to the said Thomas Talbot; also such sums as may be due to said Eli Talbot by Erwin, McLaughlin & Co, secured by Hunt, Winn & Parish; also the amt of Charles Dibrells account to said Eli Talbot.   E. Talbot   Wit: J. O. Cummins
    Thomas Talbot of Hill and Others   Registered May 18, 1821
We the undersigned, Thomas Hill, Felix Robertson and Robert H. Adams, being

by the said Eli Talbot constituted his trustees by a certain deed of trust executed to us dated the 29th May 1819, confirm the foregoing deed or conveyance of property therein described by the said Eli Talbot to Thomas Talbot the said deed of trust investing us with power and authority to make sale of all and singular the effects of the said Eli Talbot mentioned and of the settlement of his business in general. 26 July 1820 Th. Hill   Felix Robertson   Robt H. Adams
- July Sessions 1820 This Indenture of Bargain and sale was acknowledged by the said Eli Talbot to be his act and ordered to be register; also attached to said deed is a transfer and relinquishment by Thomas Hill, Felix Robertson and Robert H. Adams of the one part to Thomas Talbot of the other part and was acknowledged by Thomas Hall, Felix and Robert H. to be their act and deed and ordered to be registered.[pp458-461]

HYDE, Jordon   Bill of Sale   19 May 1821
This Indenture made 6 Dec. 1820 between Stephen Cantrell and Washington L. Hannum Trustees of the one part and Jordon Hyde of the other part. Heretofore for the purpose of securing payment of debts due the Nashville Bank, The Branch Bank of the State of Tennessee at Nashville and the Farmers and Mechanics Bank by John Stump and John S. Cox, merchants in trade under the firm of *Stump & Cox*; John Stump by his indenture dated 23 March 1819 conveyed to parties first named together with Robert Searcy, Deceased as trustees for the use of said banks among other property several negroes and the said trustees did on 19 Nov. 1819 expose to public sale in the town of Nashville part of said negroes so conveyed and at the above named time and place Jordon Hyde became the purchaser of a negro girl named Milly and now the said Stephen Cantrell and Washington L. Hannum by virtue of their authority as trustees convey said girl Milley to Jordon Hyde. 6 Dec. 1820
 Stephen Cantrell   Was. S. Hannum
- January Sessions This bill of sale was acknowledged by Stephen Cantrell and Washington L. Hannum to be their act and deed as trustees and ordered to be registered. [pp462/463]

McNAIRY, Nathaniel A.   Deed of Mortgage   19 May 1821
I, Willie Barrow, transfer to Nathaniel A. McNairy the following negroes: one negro man named Peter about thirty years of age; one boy, Egbert, ten years old; one boy, Lewis, eight years old; one boy, Aron, five years old. I have this day executed to N. A. McNairy my note due Jan. 1828, witnessed by F. Robertson and Th. Hill. If debt is paid this conveyance to be void. It is agreed that the negroes may remain in the possession of W. Barrow. 27 Jan. 1821 W. Barrow
 Wit: Felix Robertson, Th. Hill
- January Sessions This deed of mortgage was acknowledged by Willie Barrow to be his act and deed and ordered to be registered. [pp463/464]

REDDING, Augustus   Bill of Sale   19 May 1821
I, Iredale Redding have sold to Augustus Redding a certain negro woman called Jude of the age of twenty six years. 7 April 1821   Iredale Redding
Wit: Hardy S. Bryan, Alfred S. Redding
  - April Sessions This bill of sale was proven by the oath of Hardy S. Bryan and Alfred S. Redding and ordered to be registered. [p464]

HAMMOND, Eli   Bill of Sale   19 May 1821
I, William P. Owen, have sold to Eli Hammond of the county of Madison and State of Alabama seven negro slaves: Patty, Ned, Alfred, Charlotte, Jim, Edmond and Tempy, which said negroes are now in the hands of Bennet Blackman and suit is now depending in the circuit court at Nashville between said Blackman and myself for the right of said negroes.
5 Feby 1821 Will. P. Owen   Wit: Nathan Ewing, Henry Ewing
 - April Sessions This bill of sale was proven by the oath of Nathan Ewing and Henry Ewing and ordered to be registered. [p465]

PROWELL, Thomas   Bill of Sale   19 May 1821
I, Sampson Prowell, have sold to Thomas Prowell two negroes, Joe and Davison. 6 September 1820   Sampson Prowell
Test: James Thompson, William Dunnegan, Thos. Prowell
 - April Sessions This bill of sale was acknowledged by Sampson Prowell to be his act and deed and ordered to be registered. [pp465/466]

HILL, William   Deed of Mortgage   19 May 1821
I, Jordon Sandy, have sold to William Hill one feather bed and furniture, one bay mare, all my stock of cattle and hoggs, one mans saddle. Jordan Sandy is indebted to William Hill for the boarding and raising his three children until they become free or marry as the case may be for the purpose of securing the payment of said boarding . If said Jordon shall pay and satisfy said boarding this conveyance to be void. 1 January 1821   Jordon (X) Sandy
 - April Sessions This deed of mortgage was acknowledged by the said Jordon Sandy to be his act and ordered to be registered. [pp466/467]

DOUGHERTY, William   Deed of Mortgage   21 May 1821
I Michael McBride, have sold to William Dougherty the following: two bedsteads, two pair of sheets, nine windsor chairs, two sets of knives and forks, two dozen of crockery ware, two tables, three cows, 7 benches and counter, three small kegs, three coffeepots, one gridiron, one skillet, one pot, one barrel of flour and one barrel of meal, one barrel of apples and many other small articles of household furniture. If debt and interest are paid, this conveyance to be void. 30 March 1821 M. McBride
 - April Sessions This deed of mortgage was acknowledged by Michael

McBride to be his act and ordered to be registered. [pp467/469]

BARROW, Willie   Deed of Trust   30 May 1821
I, Archibald McNeill, sell to Willie Barrow - In Trust - the following: all the property, household and kitchen furniture now possessed by the said Archibald in his dwelling house and storehouse to secure the following: Archibald and George McNeill have executed notes payable to James Crawford and Andrew Napier of the City of New York, trading under the firm of *James Crawford and Co.* I hereby appoint Willie Barrow my lawful attorney to do every necessary thing to fulfil the trust. Schedule attached 24 May 1821   Arch. McNeill
Test: Th. Hill, Felix Robertson
 - May Term   This deed of trust was acknowledge by Archibald McNeill and ordered to be certified for registration. [pp469-471]
Schedule - one mahogany sideboard with white marble legs and bronze feet, one mahogany sopha with gilt and bronze feet, 12 mahogany chairs with bronze feet, two large gilt frame looking glasses, ten gilt framed looking glasses, pictures, one white alabaster clock with two ornaments of the same kind, one set scarlet moreen window curtains fringed and with gilt ornaments complete for four windows, one Brussels carpet and carpeting containing with the bordering about 120 yds, one imperial hearth rug, one large bedstead with two carved mahogany posts, one mahogany field bedstead, one pair card tables, gilt ornamented with covers for both, one rosewood work table, gilt ornamented legs and feet, one mahogany toilet or dressing table & glass, one set scarlet moreen bed curtains, fringed with gilt ornaments complete, two sets dimity bed curtains fringed complete, 4 dimity window curtains, fringed, three ingrained carpets assorted sizes, one brussels hearth rug, two pairs brass andirons, two pair shovel and tongs, three brass wire fenders, ten dozen brass carpet stair rods, two pair plated salts with cut glasses, two pair plated bottle stands, four pair plated candlesticks, one pair plated snuffers and tray, one plated twelve inch waiter, one plated tea urn, one plated bread or cake basket, two sets japanned tea trays, two dozen white handled ivory knives and forks, two cream ground gold bordered bread baskets, one plated castor of 8 bottles with gilt eagle ornament, one and one half dizen silver tablespoons, one dozen silver desert spoons, one dozen silver teaspoons, one third dizen silver salt spoons, one silver soup ladle, pair silver sugar tongs, two silver goblets, one pair two quart cut glass pitchers, set cut glass dishes containing five pieces, one dozen cut glass jelly glasses, four cut glass quart decanters, one dozen cut glass tumblers, one dozen cut glass wine glasses, one set tea china, fine, rose painted and green borders, one set blue printed dining ware, landscape patters, one dozen lemonade glasses, four foot benches covered with carpeting, one dozen white fancy chairs, one half dozen blue chairs, one morocco work box, one cordial stand, two white fancy washstands, one set dining tables, two common china presses, one candlestand, two mahogany frame looking glasses, five featherbeds, and one hair mattress

with ten large rose blankets, two common toilet tables with glasses, three teakettles, one bell mettle kettle, two common bedsteads, one chicken coop, ten pots, skillets, ovens and kettles, one gridiron, three pails and one frying pay, one churn and two kitchen tables, one white merseilles quilt, five white counterpanes, one scarlet moreen counterpane, two green venetian window b inds. [pp469-472]

FOSTER, Ephraim H.   Bill of Sale   1 June 1821
I have this day sold to Ephraim H. Foster two negro slaves: negro Jerry of dark complexion and stout made, about thirty years of age, a bricklayer by trade; negro Jim, of somewhat light complexion of middle statue, about thirty years of age, a brick maker by trade. 15 March 1820 Felix Grundy
Test: James H. Foster
- May Term 1820 This bill of sale was acknowledged by Felix Grundy and ordered to be registered. [p472]

WHITESIDE, Jinken   Bill of Sale   2 June 1821
I Exum P. Sumner, have sold to J. Whiteside one male negro slave named Jessee, thirty three years of age. 6 June 1820   Exum P. Sumner
Test: E. Pritchett   J. Philips
- May Term This bill of sale was proven by the oaths of Ephraim Pritchett and Joseph Philips and ordered to be certified for registration. [p473]

SEARCY, Robert   Bill of Sale   4 June 1821
Whereas on the 1st day of July 1819 Dan'l McGantly and John McGantly recovered a judgment in the Circuit Court of the United States at Nashville against John P. Erwin, judgment was levied against sundry household furniture and also five negroes ... on 23 May 1820 a writ was issued and levy commanding Robert Purdy, Marshal of the District of West Tennessee to expose to public sale said goods and chattels and by his Deputy, Joel M. Smith, did on 9 June 1820 and at which sale Robert Searcy by his agent Orville H. Searcy being the highest bidder became the purchaser of the following: one negro boy Thomas; one girl, Maria; one boy, Squire; one girl child, Rose; one pianoforte, one violin, one mantle clock and mantle ornaments, one bookcase, two card tables, one work stand, one small secretary, one large chair, one piano stool, two dozen windsor chairs, one new carpet, sundry music books, one old carpet, one pair looking glasses, 6 pictures, one pair andirons, one pair shovel & tongs, two fenders, one hearth rug, four beds, bedsteads and clothing, one bureau, one writing desk and drawers, one press, sundry glass and chinaware for table furniture, crockeryware, three sets knives & forks, 2 dozen silver table spoons, 2 dozen tea & desert spoons, silver ladle, one set dining table, one large map and sundry kitchen furniture, also sundry books - 20 Vol. Encyclopedia, 8 Vol Rollins Ancient History; 8 Vols, Shakespears plays, 14 Vols *Massachusetts Reports,* 7 Vols

Bacons Abridgement, 9 Vols *Branch's Reports,* 6 Vols *American Law Journal,* 2 Vol *American Digest,* 3 Vols *Chitty's Pleading,* 4 Vols *Chittys Criminal Law,* 2 Vols *Comyn on Contracts,* 16 Vols *Easts Reports,* 5 Vols *Jacobs Law Dictionary,* one large Bible, *2 Vols Tennessee Reports, Roberts on Fraud,* 4 Vols *Blackstones Commentaries,* 12 Vol *American State Papers, Mitfords Pleading, Tidds Practice, Williams Law Dictionary, Commericial Dictionary, Gillies History, Campbells Rhetoric,*4 Vols *Rollins Belle Lettres, Life of Sir William Jones, Court of Berlin.* 9 June 1820

Rob. Purdy, Marshal, W. Ten.

- May Term 1821 This indenture of bargain and sale was acknowledged by Robert Purdy, Marshal and ordered to be registered. [pp473-475]

WHITESIDE, Jenken   Deed of Mortgage   4 June 1821
I, James Crow, have sold to Jenken Whiteside one wagon and gear for four horses, three head of horses, 3 beds and bedsteads and the furniture and one chest now in my house, 12 head of black cattle, eight head of sheep and nine head of hogs, being all the cattle, sheep and hogs in my possession and three plows. James Crow is indebted to Whiteside and if the debt is paid this conveyance to be void. 12 Feb. 1821 James (X) Crow
Wit: Wm Quarles, Willo. Williams
- April Sessions This deed of mortgage was proven by the oath of William Quarles and Willo. Williams and ordered to be registered. [pp475/476]

MacDONALD & RIDGELEY   Bill of Sale   5 June 1821
This Indenture between Alexander MacDonald and Nicholas G. Ridgeley, merchants of Baltimore in the State of Maryland using the name of McDonald and Ridgeley on the one part and Josiah Horton, Sheriff of the county of Davidson and State of Tennessee. At the November Term of the Circuit Court for the County of Davidson, Felix Staggs recovered judgment against Alpha Kingsley; also Edward Bonderant at the same term recovered judgment against Kingsley; also Moses Chambers at the same term recovered judgment; also Howell Tatum at the October Sessions of the Court of Pleas and Quarter Sessions 1819; also Lot Pugh at January Sessions recovered judgment against Kingsley and whereas writs have been issued upon all said judgments to the sheriff of Davidson county against goods and chattels of Kingsley and have been levied upon two negro slaves, one boy named Isam and a woman named Jenney as well as books, household furniture and other property and exposed to public sale on 2 April 1821 at the dwelling house of the said Kingsley and McDonald and Ridgeley became the purchaser. 3 April 1820

J. Horton, Shff of Davidson County   Test: E. H. Foster, W. Cooper

Schedule of property: 1 Sideboard, 1 mahogany framed sofa, 1 breakfast table, Marshalls *Life of Washington*, 40 Windsor chairs, 1 candlestand, 1 floor carpet,

2 demijohns & 1 dozen bottles, 1 brass fender, 3 pair andirons, 3 shovel & tongs, 1 set of mantle ornaments, 1 pr of plated snuffers, 1 set of tea china, 7 best Decanters, 2 dozen tumblers, 2 dozen wine glasses & 3 goblets, 1 negro boy named Isam, 1 negro woman named Jenney, 1 beds & furniture, 1 table & washstand, 1 pitcher & bowl, 1 looking glass, 1 wash stand & table, 1 china press, 1 table, 1 washstand, 1 toilette table & glass, pitcher & bowl, 2 tables, looking glass, bowl & pitcher, 1 passage carpet, 3 family portraits,2 pr hand bellows, 1 set of dining tables, 1 china press, 1 sugar chest, 1 floor carpet, 1 hearthrug, andirons, shovel & tongs, 1 Snidle carpet, 1 broken set of liverpool dining china, 4 china pitchers, 8 teaboards & waiters, candlesticks, knifebox & snuffers, 8 tablecloths, 1 broken set of tea china, coffee cups & saucers, 1 table caster, 5 dozen knives & forks, 3 carving knives & forks, 1 table & glass bowl & pitcher, kitchen furniture, dish covers, 4000 lbs bacon, 2 cows, *Spectator - 8* volumes, *Sterns Works* - 5 volumes, *Tom Jones* - 4 volumes, several books & pamphlets, 1 barrel whiskey, Rollins *Ancient History*, 1 looking glass, *Plutarchs Lives* - 8 volumes, *Don Quixotte*, Classical Distionary, 1 set mantle ornaments, 1 looking glass, 1 carpet, 1 cow, *Shakespears Works*, 2 dozen table spoons, 2 dozen teaspoons, 1 set broken china, patent lamp.
- May 1821 The foregoing bill of sale was acknowledged by Josiah Horton, Sheriff and ordered to be registered. [pp476-481]

NICHOLS, Sarah   Bill of Sale   12 June 1821
I, Alfred Nichols have this day sold to Sarah Nichols a certain negro girl named Hannah, about fifteen years of age. 19 April 1819   A. Nichols
Test: John Nichols, Frederick Taylor
- Williamson County Circuit Court - Feb. Term 1821   I, William Smith, clerk of the Circuit Court for the county of Williamson do certify that the within deed from Alfred Nichols to Sarah Nichols was produced and proved by the oath of John Nichols and ordered to be certified that it may be registered.
- Davidson County Circuit Court - Nov. Term 1819 This bill of sale was proved by the oath of Frederick Taylor and ordered to be certified. [p481]

HOOPER, Absalom   Bill of Sale   23 July 1821
I certify that I, Nimrod Hooper, have this day sold to Absalom Hooper a negro girl named Sophy, aged eight years. 5 Feb. 1819   N. Hooper
Test: J. Hooper, Alfred Mold
- July Sessions This bill of sale was acknowledged by the said Nimrod Hooper and ordered to be registered. [p482]

HOOPER, Nimrod   Bill of Sale   23 July 1821
I, John Beazley, Constable for the County of Davidson, did this day expose to sale a yellow negro woman named Lucy, the property of Nimrod Hooper, about

22 years of age, taken as the property of Nimrod Hooper at the instance of Absalom and Joseph Hooper, and the said Absalom Hooper did purchase said girl, Lucy, he being the highest bidder. 11 July 1820 John Beazley, Constable - July Sessions This bill of sale was acknowledged by the said John Beazley, Constable, and ordered to be registered. [p482]

LUCAS, Isaac   Bill of Sale   23 July 1821
I, John Beasley, Constable of Davidson County, have this day sold a negro boy, named Dave, aged 22 years, the property of Nimrod Hooper, by virtue of five executions at the instance of Joseph and Absalom Hooper and Isaac Lucas being the highest bidder, became the purchaser. 22 Sept 1820   John Beazley - July Sessions This bill of sale was acknowledged by the said John Beazley to be his acty and ordered to be registered. [p483] assignment Lucas to A. Hooper not proved

HART, Samuel   Bill of Sale   16 Aug. 1821
I, Thomas Talbot, have sold to Samuel Hart a certain negro boy slave named Henry, about seventeen years of age. 24 July 1821   Thomas Talbot
Test: Ja. H. Talbot, Tom. Read
- July Sessions This bill of sale was acknowledged by Thomas Talbot to be his act and ordered to be registered. [p484]

HARRIS, William, Junr   Bill of Sale   16 Aug. 1821
I, Howell Harris, have this day given to William Harris, Junr, on account of the esteem and particular regard that I have for him, a negro boy named Grig.
18 June 1821   Howell Harris   Wit: William Brown, Edwin Harriss
- July Sessions This bill of sale was acknowledged by Howell Harris to be his act and ordered to be registered. [p484]

HARRIS, Elizabeth   Bill of Sale   16 Aug. 1821
I, Howell Harris, have this day given to Elizabeth Harris on account of the esteem that I have for her, two negroes; one negro woman named Nance, one boy named Jacob, Nance' son. 18 June 1821   Howell Harris
Test: William Brown, Edwin Harris
- This bill of sale was acknowledged by Howell Harris to be his act and ordered to be registered. [p485]

HARRIS, Sally   Bill of Sale   16 Aug. 1821
I, Howell Harris, have this day given to Sally Harris on account of the esteem and particular regard that I have for her, a certain negro woman, named Rhody.
18 June 1821   Howell Harris   Test: William Brown, Edwin Harris
- July Sessions   This bill of sale was acknowledged by Howell Harris and ordered to be registered. [p486]

COMPTON, William   Bill of Sale   16 August 1821
I have sold to William Compton two negro girls named Rhoda and Fanny, the first aged about thirteen years and the latter aged about eighteen heretofore delivered by Thos. H. Fletcher for me to William Compton. Fanny has had a girl child which is hereby conveyed and sold. 16 July 1821 John McNairy
Test: Tho. H. Fletcher, R. Sanderson
 - July Sessions This bill of sale was proven by the oaths of Thomas H. Fletcher and Robert Sanderson and ordered to be registered. [p486]

COMPTON, William   Bill of Sale   16 August 1821
I, Sam'l B. Marshall, have sold to William Compton certain negro slave named Dave, aged about twenty four years. 28 Oct. 1820   Sam. B. Marshall
Test: John Marshall
 - July Sessions This bill of sale was proven by the oath of John Marshall and ordered to be registered. [p487]

FOSTER, Ephraim H.   Deed of Trust   16 August 1821
Wilkin Tannehill has conveyed to Ephraim H. Foster the following named property: Sundry books [a very large & varied library is listed volume by volume] 6 chairs, 1 settee, 1 bedstead, bed & clothing, one clothespress, one liquor case, one work stand ... Wilkins Tannehill is indebted to Ephraim H. Foster by notes - if debt is paid, this deed to be void. 26 Oct. 1822   W. Tannehill Test: Geo. Shall, Step'n Cantrell
 - District of West Tennessee - I, Nathaniel A. McNairy, Clerk of the Court of the United States for the District of West Tennessee certify the within trust was proven in open court by George Shall and Stephen Cantrell and ordered to be certified. 26 June 1821 [pp 487-499]

WILKINSON, William, Junr   Deed of Trust   16 August 1821
I, Henry Douglass, convey to William Wilkinson, Junr the following property: one negro man named Jack, about thirty years old, of black complexion, now under the care and in the possession of Dr.. Thomas Richmond of Wilson County who is treating him for an ulcer on the arm; one negro woman called Zella, about twenty five years of age, of dark complexion, now in possession of my son in law, James Boon; one curtain bedstead, one bed, six cotton sheets, six counterpanes, two white and four checked, eight rose blankets, four quilts, one bureau, one dining table, one dressing table, six common chairs, one candlestand, one pair fire dogs, one looking glass, four waiters, one set silver teaspoons, one cradle and furniture, one side saddle, one frying pan, two ovens, two pots, two pails, one pair waffle irons, one patent coffeemill, one pot rack, one pair shovel & tongs, one sugarbox, two crocks or jars, one trundle bed and bedstead. In Trust - If Henry shall pay debt this deed to be void. 19 Feb. 1821
 Henry Douglas   Test: Ephraim H. Foster, Wm Arthur

- July Sessions This deed of trust was proven by the oaths of Ephraim H. Foster and William Arthur and ordered to be registered. [pp490-492]

CHERRY, Eli   Bill of Sale   17 August 1821
I, Darling Cherry, have sold to Eli Cherry two negroes, one woman and child by names Edy and Silvey, one about twenty years old and the other about six years old. 2 February 1821   Darling Cherry
Test: Stranhorn Mank, Robert W. Green, W. S. Green, Lem'l Kennedy
- July Sessions This bill of sale was proven by the oath of Robert W. Green and Lemuel Kennedy and ordered to be registered. [p492]

CROW, William L.   Bill of Sale   17 August 1821
I, James Crow, have sold to William L. Crow a negro boy named Milan, ten years old/. 24 February 1821   James (X) Crow
Test: John Gowin, W. H. McLaughlin
- July Sessions This bill of sale was acknowledged by James Crow to be his act and ordered to be registered. [p493]

FITZHUGH, John   Bill of Sale   17 August 1821
I, Bennet Blackman of Maury County and State of Tennessee, have sold to John Fitzhugh a certain negro man aged about twenty one years, by the name of Herrod. 3 Feb'y 1821   Bennet Blackman
Witness: Charles Hays, Henry Ewing
- This bill of sale was acknowledged by Bennet Blackman to be his act and ordered to be registered. [p493]

IRWIN, James   Bill of Sale   17 August 1821
I, John Hail of Simpson County, Kentucky, have sold to James Irwin a female slave particularly mentioned in the attached schedule: one mulatto woman named Liza, aged about thirty nine years, late in the possession of said John Hail.
17 July 1821   John Hail   Test: Jno B. West
- July Sessions This bill of sale was proven by the oath of John B. West and ordered to be registered. [p494]

McCASLAND, William   Bill of Sale   17 August 1821
This day I have sold to William McCasland a negro woman by the name of Amrchy, aged about twenty one. 22 May 1821   David Logue   Test:
Thomas Powell, Wm P. Byrn
- July Sessions This bill of sale was acknowledged by David Logue to be his act and ordered to be registered. [p495]

BARRY, Richard H.   Bill of Sale   17 August 1821
This day received of Rich'd H. Barry two hundred and fifty dollars in full for my

125

part of the estate willed to me by my Grandfather, Frederick Stump .... I do furthermore transfer all my claim to said estate to the said Rich. H. Barry.
  Feb'y 15, 1821   John Stump, Junr
Test: Jno Criddle, Robert Lanier
 - July Sessions This bill of Sale was proven by the oaths of John Criddle and Robert Lanier and ordered to be registered. [p495]

McDONALD, William N. T.   Deed of Gift   22 August 1821
I, Daniel McDonald, in consideration of the love, good will and affection which I have and do bear toward my loving son William N. T. McDonald, do give unto the said William N. T. McDonald all my goods and chattles not being in my possession. To wit, one negro by the name of Will and one named Lydia, and one by the name of Meriah, and one by the name of Limbreck, and one by the name of Old Hannah, one by the name of little Dinah; all my cattle, hoggs and horses and household and kitchen furniture and also all my crib of corn.
12 February 1821   Daniel McDana
Test: Lewis Dunn, Wm S. Gordon, Jas. Lovell
 - July Sessions This Deed of Gift was proven by the oath of James Lovell and William S. Gordon and ordered to be registered. [p496]

INDEX

132

140

144

slave

153

154